Mastering Tennis Trading

Essential analysis and winning strategies to
give you an edge in online tennis trading

By Daniel Weston

HARRIMAN HOUSE LTD

18 College Street

Petersfield

Hampshire

GU31 4AD

GREAT BRITAIN

Tel: +44 (0)1730 233870

Email: contact@harriman-house.com

Website: www.harriman-house.com

First published in Great Britain in 2015

Copyright © Harriman House

The right of Daniel Weston to be identified as the Author has been asserted in accordance with the Copyright, Designs and Patents Act 1988.

ISBN: 978-0-85719-499-2

British Library Cataloguing in Publication Data

A CIP catalogue record for this book can be obtained from the British Library.

Preface

Tennis is the second biggest sport for in-play turnover in the betting markets, so it is clear that it offers fantastic potential for educated, professional traders to achieve high levels of profits. This book gives the reader the tools to take a calm, strategic approach to tennis trading – in contrast to the emotional, impulsive trading style of many – and this will give you an edge in the markets.

A tennis trader's goal is to take advantage of the fluctuations of the two players odds' for winning a match, which vary prior to and, particularly, during the match. As in-play events cause mispricing and overreactions in the market, they swing the prices in different directions. Traders seek to make a profit based on being able to correctly anticipate these fluctuations.

As a tennis trading analyst and owner of **www.tennisratings.co.uk**, as well as the tennis writer for **www.pinnaclesports.com**, I have vast experience and knowledge of the in-play statistics behind tennis. As I carry out my analysis, a constant source of frustration to me is the myths and subjective analysis in the media and social media. Eventually my frustration turned to inspiration and I decided to take a stand against these fallacies. I therefore decided to write this book with the intention of improving readers' tennis trading and to try and eradicate many of the mistruths that are frequently presented.

This book will help you learn tennis trading strategies for the in-play markets on the online betting exchanges – notably Betfair and Betdaq. The strategies presented will help you to add statistically-proven techniques to your trading armoury and assist you in creating a professional, organised trading script which will prevent a haphazard, impulsive and purely gambling trading style.

It will help readers in basic areas such as a trading set-up and how to avoid technological issues, to more advanced subjects such as assessing which trading strategies work best and which entry points provide the best risk/reward ratios, as well as avoiding specific danger points which will help to eradicate costly losses. The statistics – compiled over many hours of analysis – and strategies will open your eyes to the possibilities in the in-play tennis markets.

If you're beginning your trading journey, or have some experience but are looking for a book with a statistical analysis on a variety of tennis trading subjects and strategies, this is the book for you. I also provide viable trading strategies and thought-provoking ideas which will allow your tennis trading to improve enough to earn you a part-time income, or to eventually allow you to turn full-time once you have gained enough experience.

If you're an experienced tennis trader that's looking for some different angles to approach what you already do well, then this is also the right book for you.

Writing this book has been fun. I truly hope that you will enjoy reading it and that its content can help to earn you additional future profits, or even just avoid future losses by eradicating some basic mistakes. I am confident that it will do so.

Having said that, please be aware that as a form of gambling, tennis trading has risk attached to it. All gambling, no matter how big an edge you have, carries this element of risk. All bets and trades are made at your own risk.

If you have any questions about the handbook, or any questions related to tennis trading, please feel free to contact me at **tennistrades@gmail. com** and I will get back to you as soon as possible.

Free eBook with every print book purchase. Visit:

ebooks.harriman-house.com/masteringtennistrading

for more information.

Contents

Introduction To Tennis Trading

SETUP

Hardware

ALL TENNIS TRADERS NEED A DEVICE TO TRADE from, such as a computer. Personally I wouldn't recommend trading with a phone or tablet as your main device as the refresh rates (the speed at which the prices and available back/lay sums refresh on the device) are slower and there aren't as many options or functions available as on a computer (e.g. there is no price graph on the iPhone). As a last resort handheld devices can be a useful backup if your computer is having technical problems.

What I have as backup is the following:

* An iPad and iPhone if my computer unexpectedly breaks.

* A 3G connection on my iPhone in case my internet goes down.

* Another exchange or bookmaker account in case Betfair goes down.

I really would recommend having all three of these in case of technological failure. With trading, often our stake is a lot bigger than our stop-loss figure, so a loss of a full stake can be disastrous. Having these back-up solutions will ensure that this disaster does not happen.

Software

I don't use third-party software (also known as **API applications**). These software applications allow users to sign into their Betfair account and use the applications' software to trade and in some cases automate your trading. Features include a faster refresh rate and the ability to build in a stop-loss position (a worst-case position where the software trades out if the trade goes against you). They are useful but I have always just used the Betfair interface and have been fine with doing so. The API applications are especially useful, however, if you trade during individual games.

Keeping track of matches

It's important for new traders to realise that *live* match pictures may not necessarily be live. Pictures on television, whether on terrestrial TV or satellite, are subject to at least a five-second delay. It's worth noting that the Betfair live stream is actually several seconds faster than live TV. However, I would recommend refreshing your Betfair stream periodically because it can fall behind by several seconds, particularly if you don't have the fastest computer or internet connection and are streaming several matches at the same time.

For trading non-live matches (those which aren't broadcast live on television or streamed via betting sites), in my experience the best live score website is **www.flashscores.co.uk**. It's marginally quicker than the other live score websites available and I particularly like the My Games tab (available on the top right-hand side of the toolbar on the main screen) where you can add the matches you want to follow and focus on those.

Your stake

Regarding your stake, I would strongly recommend you start small when you first begin tennis trading. If you cannot win in the long term with small stakes, you won't win with larger stakes either – you'll just lose more money.

There's no shame in starting small and working your way up gradually when you get more confidence and experience with your strategies and the market. This will be discussed further in the Bankroll Management chapter.

BASIC INFORMATION AND MARKET THOUGHTS

Cross-matching

As we should all be aware, tennis is a simple sport. There are two outcomes – either one player wins or the other does. What that means for the trading/betting markets is that one player is always going to be odds on (1.xx) in price – the favourite.

Unlike in other sports that have a number of outcomes, tennis trading on Betfair employs **cross-matching**. What this essentially means is that you can back either player and you will get the guaranteed best price – effectively if you back the underdog, the software can **lay** the favourite if it provides you with a price advantage. This means you don't have to worry about liquidity on a single player, you can trade either player equally.

Whilst we are on the subject of Betfair rules, it's important for all traders to know that if the first set is not completed, all bets are voided. Once the first set is completed, all bets stand in the event of a retirement.

Laying

Some readers may be wondering what a **lay** of a player means. If you lay a player, you are effectively, at that point, backing them to lose. This does not mean we are necessarily looking for that to happen as the final outcome. What we are looking to achieve is for that player's price to increase, so we can trade out of our position for a guaranteed profit no matter who wins.

For those of you who are still unclear, the following illustration should be of help.

Match Odds - Matched: GBP 20			M	Going In-Play	Rules	
			Back	Lay		
🐎 Tatsuma Ito	2.66	3.6	3.85	3.95	4.1	990
	£19	£44	£43	£42	£97	£2
🐎 Igor Sijsling	1.06	1.33	1.34	1.35	1.38	1.6
	£10	£300	£124	£123	£115	£33

Here you can see the Betfair market for the match between Tatsuma Ito and Igor Sijsling. The furthest right price under the 'Back' column is the currently available price to back – in Sijslings's case 1.34. The furthest left price under the 'Lay' column is the currently available price to lay – so here for Sijsling it is 1.35.

Therefore if we backed Sijsling for £100 our potential profit, should he win, would be **£34**.

However, should we feel the Sijsling price is likely to rise then we would want to lay Sijsling at 1.35. If we want to lay Sijsling for £100, our liability would be £35 (£100*0.35).

It is important to note here that when you back a player, your liability is your stake (in this instance £100), but when you lay a player your liability is the backer's stake (in this instance £100) multiplied by the price minus 1. In this case 1.35-1 = 0.35 and multiplying by £100 gives £35.

This screen also shows you how much you can currently bet on each outcome. In the column where the price of 1.34 is given for backing Sijsling, we can see that below this price is the figure £124. This means you can back Sijsling at 1.34 for £124. The figures to the left show how much you can currently bet at other prices. Should you wish to back Sijsling for more than £124, you can back him at 1.33 for £300.

Should we lay Sijsling for £100 at 1.35 pre-match, and his price rises to 2.00 during the match, you can hedge for profit in several ways. Firstly, it is then possible to back Sijsling for £100, enabling us to generate £65 profit on Sijsling if he wins, and £0 profit or loss on Ito. It is also possible for us to equally hedge our position, backing Sijsling for £67.50, enabling us to generate £32.50 profit on both players. In both situations, we cannot lose regardless of which player wins the match. Furthermore, in the second example, we have equal profit on both players, so we win no matter who eventually wins the match.

Liquidity

As a rule of thumb, live video matches on Betfair have good liquidity where you can get large trades matched. The matches without live video tend to be fairly mixed in terms of liquidity – it usually depends on the names of the players whether the market will be liquid or not. The more famous they are, or the bigger the match, the more likely it is there will be good liquidity in the market. Ideally you'd want to have at least £30,000 to £40,000 matched in the match odds market – shown on the Betfair screen for each match – before the match starts for it to be a viable candidate to trade in-play.

This is particularly relevant when your stakes are reasonably high and also if you want to trade points in-game. I'd only recommend live streamed matches where at least £100,000 is matched (or it's on a high profile television channel) if you want to trade points in-game.

The reason why you need a market to be fairly liquid is because you need to be sure you can exit the market when you want to. If you can't get your stake matched easily to get out of the market then you could find yourself having to take very poor prices just to try and salvage some of your stake should the match turn against you.

Lay low and back high

The basic premise of trading is to **lay low and back high**, or vice versa. However, I want to add more thoughts to that because people's interpretations of 'low' and 'high' can be vastly different.

I generally don't back a player unless the trade is very short-term (for example an individual service game) when their price is odds on (under 2.00) on Betfair. The downside is just too large compared to the potential reward.

Risk/reward is a theme of trading and you will see I refer to it numerous times. Should you back a player at odds-on (under 2.00), if the match moves against you, you risk the price passing through points when the tick increments increase, increasing your loss per tick significantly (see below).

The Betfair tick increment system is shown in the following table.

BETFAIR PRICE INCREMENT SYSTEM

Price	Tick per unit price increment	Example
1.00-2.00	One tick per one unit price increment	1.01 to 1.02 is one tick
2.00-3.00	One tick per two unit price increment	2.00 to 2.02 is one tick – i.e. a price of 2.01 is unavailable
3.00-4.00	One tick per five unit price increment	3.00 to 3.05 is one tick
4.00-6.00	One tick per ten unit price increment	4.00 to 4.10 is one tick
6.00-10.00	One tick per 20 unit price increment	6.00 to 6.20 is one tick
10.00-20.00	One tick per 50 unit price increment	10.00 to 10.50 is one tick
20.00-30.00	One tick per 100 unit price increment	20.00 to 21.00 is one tick
30.00-50.00	One tick per 200 unit price increment	30.00 to 32.00 is one tick
50.00-100.00	One tick per 500 unit price increment	50.00 to 55.00 is one tick
100.00-1000.00	One tick per 1000 unit price increment	100.00 to 110.00 is one tick

In-play markets

Generally speaking, the in-play markets fairly rigidly stick to the idea of starting prices adjusted according to the current score. Therefore, often if there is value on a player pre-match, the value on that player will also be there in-play to some extent. It often takes a significant event, such as a medical timeout for a player, to deviate from this assessment. There will be a lot more discussion on the effect of medical timeouts in the Dangerous Situations chapter.

Because the markets generally stick to the *starting prices adjusted for the current score* formula, there can often be value in various situations where some players react very differently to others. For example, some players play best in adversity and have excellent records a set down (e.g. Andy

Murray and Kirsten Flipkens), whereas others almost always give up (e.g. Michael Llodra and Arantxa Rus). Deciding sets also test the mental and physical strength of a player – and some players have a very poor record in these. There will be more on this, and some other examples of viable entry points, in later chapters.

There are various situations, such as medical timeouts, and certain scorelines, that influence the market more than others. For example, if a player wins a set 6-0 or 6-1 then their price for the match will be somewhat shorter than if they won it 7-6. Obviously that's fairly logical because the player that won the set easily has exhibited a great level of dominance over their opponent. Having said this, the records of past matches are littered with examples of players winning a set 6-0 or 6-1 and then losing the match. It's much more commonplace than many think, in both men's and women's tennis.

It's also important to realise that the price for a woman a set up should be lower than a man with the equivalent starting price. The average percentage for top 100 players winning the match after winning the first set in the WTA is 87%, but this figure reduces to 84% for the ATP in the sample I carried out.

Because of the number of variables in a tennis match, it's impossible to give an exact price change guide for a player from starting price to a set up. Generally, if you use a rule of thumb for a favourite where you divide the starting price by 4 then you won't be too far out, for example a 1.25 starting price goes to roughly 1.06 when the player is a set up. It's very useful to have a rough idea of this because it's often a natural exit point. The following example illustrates this.

Example

A player starts at 2.00 and breaks their opponent near the start of the first set. Following this break of serve, their price falls to around 1.50. For whatever reason, you decide to lay this player at around 1.50. You can do so knowing that the very worst case scenario is a 30 tick loss to about 1.20 at the end of the set. This is highly useful because you will be able to know what your maximum loss is as soon as you place the lay bet.

So – if you lay a player at 1.50 for a £100 stake, your liability would be £50. If you then have to trade out at 1.20, if you back the same player as you previously laid for £125 you have an equal £25 loss for either player.

To clarify, laying a player at 1.50 for £100 generates a liability of £50 (£100*.5).

If we have to trade out at 1.20 after the trade moves against us, we can back the player at 1.20 for £125, which generates a potential profit of £25.00 (£125*.2), leading to a net loss of £25 on either player (£25-£50).

The screenshot below illustrates this scenario.

Knowing this information in advance means you are aware that you can only lose about half your liability should the player you've laid take the first set.

Holding and breaking

Some people try and express a standard amount of ticks won or lost for a hold or break. In my experience that's impossible to quantify. I have no doubt that the market is too standard with regards to treating all players the same for holding or breaking, but you will find that the end of each set is a great deal more volatile than the start of it.

For example, you may find that at 0-0 in the first set, a hold of serve may shorten the server by as little as 8 to 10 ticks. If a player is serving for the set at 5-4, this amount could as much as quadruple simply because it's a key service game. So, trying to achieve a fixed idea of ticks won or lost for holding or breaking serve for all service games is not possible or sensible.

The market, of course, realises that the women's average service hold percentage is significantly lower than the men's. Therefore, should a WTA player hold serve, it is reasonable to expect that their price will shorten by more ticks than an ATP player, simply because the event is more unlikely. As you might expect, a break also affects the market differently – a woman breaking serve tends to move the prices less than a man breaking serve, simply because women do it more frequently.

HEDGING

Hedging is the process where we exit our trade with either a guaranteed profit or a guaranteed loss, no matter what the outcome. If our trade is going against us, we can hedge for a smaller guaranteed loss than our total liability, therefore cutting our losses without risking our full stake. If the trade is going in our favour, we can hedge for a guaranteed profit no matter what the outcome is eventually.

Due to the trading software available and the **cash out** feature now available on Betfair – where the Betfair software equally hedges your position for you – many traders, especially novice traders, hedge their positions evenly on all occasions.

I wouldn't necessarily advocate hedging evenly. Nearer the end of the match I don't have a problem with this, but in the first set especially I don't really like this approach.

For example, you back a player as you perceive them to be value in the first set when it's currently on serve. Immediately they break their opponent, leading to their price to decrease. This allows you to hedge for guaranteed profit, as shown in the first Ormaechea vs Bertens screenshot below. But why would you automatically equally hedge in this situation? If a player is perceived to be value before they break, why would they immediately not be value when they break?

In this situation, we might wish to back Ormaechea for £100 at 2.02 at the start of Bertens' service game. (Potential profit of £102: £100*1.02.)

Upon a break of serve, let's assume Ormaechea's lay price drops to 1.50. When this occurs, it is possible to equally hedge by laying Ormaechea for £134.66 at 1.50 (potential profit of £67.33: £134.66*.5).

Therefore, the equal hedge figure is £34.67 (£102-£67.33).

Perhaps a better approach in this spot would be to clear your liability on the other player, leaving all your profit on the player you previously backed. Hedging equally is actually pretty lazy and, as with any trade, you should only do it with solid reasoning.

In this situation, we simply adapt the first trade so we structure the lay bet in a slightly different way, laying Ormaechea for £100 (our original back stake), which generates potential profit of £50 (£100*.5).

Therefore, we can generate a situation where we neither win nor lose should Bertens win the match, but we make £52 if Ormaechea does (£102-£50).

Pre-match Trading

DRIFTING PRICES

I THOUGHT THAT I WOULD START OFF WITH A CHAPTER on pre-match trading. After all, what can be better than locking in a profit before the match starts?

For a player's price to move pre-match, the market needs to disagree with the opening lines that the bookmakers introduce. The opening lines at a company like Pinnacle Sports can be moved fairly easily with a few medium to large bets and the bookmaker's stake limits tend to reflect that – they're much smaller than they are nearer the match start time.

On Betfair it can be difficult to get a big trade matched very early but if you are persistent and a little flexible with your prices you should be able to get a fair sum matched eventually, especially in a high profile or live streamed match.

I feel that a lot of tennis traders, punters and pundits are often perplexed about the propensity for a player's pre-match price to drift (i.e. increase) and consider that it's guesswork whether to take an early pre-match price or wait until closer to the start of the match. However, I've done a great deal of work regarding price movements and I think that the movement is highly predictable.

The market tends to disagree with a price for one of several reasons.

WHY THE MARKET DISAGREES WITH A PRE-MATCH PRICE

The names of the players

The first reason is simply the names of the two players.

For example – a big name will always attract market interest. Caroline Wozniacki is a prime example of that. At the 2013 WTA Brussels tournament, she started her first match against Jie Zheng at 1.25. This price was insane considering her run of horrendous form, when recently she had lost to Qiang Wang, Garbine Muguruza and Stefanie Voegele, all of whom were ranked outside the top 50. Before the Zheng match she had lost her last four outings, yet you could lay her at 1.25 pre-match! That was all because of her reputation.

In the men's game, Marcos Baghdatis is a notable player. Not close to his previous ability, he is still often priced very low by the bookmakers due to his reputation. His record in the last 12 months at the time of writing is 28 wins and 25 losses – if you had blind backed him in all of those matches you would have achieved a terrible Return on Investment of -18.6%.

Andy Murray on clay is another example. His clay stats are very poor for a player of his rank – he is a great value lay on the surface. The bookmakers know they will attract attention just because of his name and therefore price him very short. At the time of writing, based on Pinnacle Sports closing prices, Murray has a career Return of Investment on clay of -16.1% and in the last year that figure is -15.5%. If you look at his record across all surfaces instead of clay Murray has a positive Return on Investment, which really illustrates how much worse he plays on clay and how he tends to be priced too short on the surface.

Mathematical hold models

The second reason that a price changes is that modellers like myself with mathematical projected hold models (based on service points/return points won or service hold/break percentages) realise that a certain price is value according to their models.

In my opinion – and I'm not alone in thinking it – this is the only way of effectively modelling a starting price based on stats. Of course, a modeller then must adjust for other matchup factors, but it is the only effective way of setting a base price for a player to start with.

Modellers tend to be either individual big hitters or work with betting syndicates and they can move the market very easily. Since I started using projected holds to predict starting prices, I've noticed that I can accurately predict which players' prices will lengthen or shorten in the market on the majority of occasions.

Information

The final reason is information. Sometimes a player leaks information on social media regarding an injury or illness that they have picked up, or have not recovered from. Sometimes they might just leak it to associates – who then can profit from that information. And of course, some matches might have strong suspicions that they are fixed. I wouldn't say that there are many matches that are suspicious, but I would say that there are some. It definitely does go on.

What always worries me pre-match is when a player is clearly no value based on my projected hold model, there is nothing leaked on social media yet their price keeps falling. That's when I get very suspicious.

DRIFT ANALYSIS OF THE 2012 SEASON

I performed starting price drift analysis of the 2012 season and found some very interesting information.

WTA anlysis

In the WTA, if you had opposed every player of the 659 that had drifted over 5% in implied odds for level stakes, you would have lost 1.52% of your stake on average each bet (based on Pinnacle Sports closing prices). So we can clearly see that the market, on the whole, corrects itself well by the start of the match.

This is because the Pinnacle Sports profit margin is generally around 3% per match, roughly split between each player. So it's reasonable to assume that each player will have around 1.5% 'juice' on them, and that if the results of a blind-backed scenario equate to a return on investment of around this figure, we can further assume the market is efficient.

There were certain players that drifted often – the stats are shown in the table below.

Player	How often drifted by more than 5%	Opening price range when drifting
Alberta Brianti	8 out of 25	1.66-3.21
Julia Cohen	7 out of 11	1.99-3.66
Eleni Daniilidou	8 out of 30 (and won in none of these 8 matches)	2.01-4.00
Marina Erakovic	10 out of 40	1.5-3.08
Stephanie Foretz-Gacon	7 out of 20	1.55-4.64
Jarmila Gajdosova	8 out of 26	1.53-3.85
Edina Gallovits-Hall	5 out of 14	1.75-3.68
Daniela Hantuchova	11 out of 47	1.26-2.60
Jelena Jankovic	13 out of 59	1.16-2.42
Mathilde Johansson	7 out of 27	1.43-3.97
Anne Keothavong	7 out of 24	1.07-3.36
Anabel Medina Garrigues	12 out of 49	1.43-3.37
Arantxa Rus	8 out of 25	1.74-5.24
Francesca Schiavone	12 out of 43	1.27-3.68
Anna Tatishvili	9 out of 34	1.25-3.78
Elena Vesnina	9 out of 31	1.32-3.31
Venus Williams	8 out of 33	1.2-2.55
Jie Zheng	12 out of 49	1.45-3.05

I'd split the majority of these players into two categories. They are either occasional WTA Tour players with fairly low rankings or very low projected hold percentages (e.g. Cohen, Rus, Tatishvili), or veterans (e.g. Hantuchova, Jankovic, Schiavone, Williams) that are possibly not in favour with the betting market due to their ability not being nearly as high as when they were at the top of their game.

ATP analysis

In the ATP, the drifting figures appear to show that the market still isn't fully corrected by the start of the match. If you had backed every ATP player that had drifted over 5% in implied odds in 2012 (674 outcomes) for level stakes you'd have a -6.48% Return on Investment (based on Pinnacle Sports closing prices).

So, because backing the drifters had such a poor return, even taking into account any profit margin from the bookmakers, if you took the best closing price on the players with odds *shortening* – the opposite approach – by over 5% pre-match you'd be looking at a reasonable profit.

As with the WTA, there were players that drifted with regularity. The table below shows the stats.

Player	How often drifted by more than 5%	Opening price range when drifting
Igor Andreev	8 out of 27	1.3-3.40
Pablo Andujar	17 out of 48	1.33-6.24
Alex Bogomolov Jr	11 out of 39	1.41-7.98
Tatsuma Ito	7 out of 22	1.55-7.48
Igor Kunitsyn	7 out of 23	1.58-4.22
Paolo Lorenzi	7 out of 25	1.83-6.58
Nicolas Mahut	9 out of 34	1.32-6.60
Eric Prodon	5 out of 7	3.01-4.91
Pere Riba	5 out of 8	2.13-6.10
Gilles Simon	14 out of 66	1.24-5.44
Joao Souza	7 out of 14	1.84-4.60
Bernard Tomic	11 out of 48	1.20-3.61
Viktor Troicki	13 out of 48	1.20-3.61
Filippo Volandri	12 out of 31	1.62-5.04

Looking at these players it's clear to see that the vast majority are journeyman Challenger Tour players that sometimes play on the ATP Tour, and when they do they generally have a mediocre record.

It's worth noting that none of the young Challenger Tour decent prospects made this list when stepping up to the ATP main tour.

Furthermore, as with the WTA, there are a lot of weak servers on this list (hence the player's projected hold will be low, leading to interest from modellers).

Certain players also shortened a great deal in the pre-match betting. The following table shows players that shortened over 5% on a regular basis in 2012.

Player	% of time shortened by more than 5% of implied odds
Brian Baker	29%
Thomaz Bellucci	22%
Julien Benneteau	22%
Ricardas Berankis	47% – small sample
James Blake	30% – small sample
Alexandr Dolgopolov	22%
Grigor Dimitrov	30%
Ryan Harrison	21%
Gael Monfils	21%
Kei Nishikori	21%
Sam Querrey	29%
Andreas Seppi	21%

I feel that with a good projected hold model and the knowledge about which players are often favoured by the market, you can accurately predict which players' prices will change in the run-up to a match. Armed with this information, traders have a fantastic chance to lock in profits before the match starts by backing a player in the knowledge that their price is likely to fall prior to the match starting. Pre-match punters have the opportunity to get maximum value for their bets, as they will be able to make an assessment as to whether the player is worth backing on opening prices, or close to the match start time.

Projected Service Holds

INTRODUCTION TO PROJECTED SERVICE HOLDS

PROJECTED SERVICE HOLDS ARE ABSOLUTELY critical to trading a match correctly. If you don't consider them, or interpret them incorrectly, then in my opinion you will not enjoy much success in tennis trading.

When calculating a projected service hold, my model will calculate court speed, the likelihood of surface holds and breaks for both players, the sample size, and relate this to the ATP or WTA mean. This gives us a pretty reliable estimate of the percentage of times a player will hold their serve and we can then relate this to the mean amount for each tour.

Some average stats (at the time of writing) are shown in the tables below:

ATP HOLD STATS

Surface	Percentage hold
All surfaces	78.3%
Indoor hard	79.2%
Hard court	78.4%
Clay	75.9%
Grass	82.8%

WTA HOLD STATS

Surface	Percentage hold
All surfaces	63.6%
Indoor hard	65.2%
Hard court	63.1%
Clay	61.6%
Grass	69.4%

An interesting initial observation from these figures is that the clay court average hold is only 2.4% below the ATP all-surfaces average, and 1.7% behind WTA all-surfaces average. This puts paid to the myth that clay courts feature many fewer holds than harder surfaces.

More important than this is that if we can reasonably calculate that a player will have a projected hold above or below these average numbers for all players then we can start to make some sort of judgement about how the match will proceed.

Two players well above the average, particularly in the men's tour, for example in the high 80%'s, will feature in a match with few breaks and will generally have a high number of games in total. Conversely, if both players have projected holds below 70% in the ATP, we can expect both players' serve to be pressurised.

Generally I use the following guidelines when considering projected service holds:

ATP

Server level	Percentage hold
Very good server	Over 85%
Good server	81-85%
Bad server	64-74%
Very bad server	Less than 64%

WTA

Server level	Percentage hold
Very good server	Over 74%
Good server	70-74%
Bad server	50-60%
Very bad server	Less than 50%

Court speed

Court speed is pretty hard to quantify in terms of the actual pace that the court is, so I quantify it based on the mean service hold compared to the ATP/WTA average. There are other ways that you can look at this as well, such as the average aces per game or average break points per game.

It's vital that you take court speed into account in your calculations. Fast courts can feature significantly fewer breaks than slower courts and even the worst servers can hold serve much more regularly on faster courts (and faster surfaces such as grass) than on slower courts.

Summary

This should give you a guideline on how to establish how a player is likely to perform and how the match is likely to go. In the next few chapters, you will begin to understand how these statistics can be applied during the course of the match to enable us to evaluate which methods to apply to the various situations we find ourselves in.

USING PROJECTED HOLD PERCENTAGES TO INFER VALUE IN-PLAY

The importance of value

Before I present any trading strategies, I need to alert readers to the importance of achieving *value* in your trades.

Some bettors appear to forget this concept when trading in-play as opposed to pre-match. They just favour a player with little reasoning as to whether the player is value or not, thinking the odds are 50/50 whether the price goes up or down.

As with pre-match betting, of course it is vital to get value for your in-play trades. If you can lay at 1.80 when the true price is 2.20, then you are getting huge value (in that case an edge of 10.1%), so it's vital to be able to assess when those situations present themselves.

As we saw in the previous section, with an effective projected hold model, we can calculate the likelihood of each player holding serve in an average service game, and can categorise a player accordingly. However, before we blindly lay all bad servers when serving and back all good servers when serving we need to consider whether we are getting value for our trades.

Whilst it's fair to say that the pre-match prices need to be significantly wrong before opposing a WTA player with a 45% projected hold does not become a value proposition, these opportunities don't present themselves very often. So we need to make a judgement on whether a player is value based on their pre-match prices.

Employing a projected hold model

As I mentioned previously, a player that is value pre-match also tends to be value in-play because the market, most of the time, will adjust a starting price based on the scoreline. So if we can find the value players pre-match, the chances are that we can find the value in-play too. And a projected hold model does just that.

Let's take the match between Benoit Paire and Kei Nishikori in the French Open 2013 as an example.

Benoit Paire versus Kei Nishikori

This match came after Paire had a superb run to the semi-finals of the Rome Masters that included wins over the higher ranked Juan Monaco and Juan Martin Del Potro. Both players started around the even money price, with Paire originally being priced as 1.88 favourite with Pinnacle Sports. The market initially was hugely in favour of Paire, taking his price down to 1.78 before an influx of smart money on Nishikori saw the prices move back towards 2.00.

However, I felt that Paire was priced as a false favourite originally by the bookmakers due to his perceived good form. My projected hold model also was against Paire. It was interesting to see that his serve and return stats during the 'run of form' were barely an improvement on his three-month clay stats. This would also indicate that he was too short in the markets.

I had other reasons for thinking that the price on Paire was flawed too. Firstly, in that run of six wins from seven matches, Paire only beat two players when underdog – those already named above. Furthermore, Del Potro was severely out of sorts in that victory for Paire and withdrew from the French Open subsequently.

Finally, it's important to realise that form is often just positive variance. A player is often perceived to be in form but actually might have won a couple of very tight matches where several key shots hit the line instead of them being an inch out. Or, as in the case of Paire, a player may have played a big name player that severely underperformed on the day and got too much credit for the victory.

In this case, Paire's apparent 'form' was way too deep in the thoughts of both the bookmakers and the gamblers, leaving superb value on Nishikori.

Projected holds had Paire at 64.4% and Nishikori significantly higher at 79.2%. After making several small adjustments for situational factors, this gave Nishikori a modelled starting price of 1.57 – huge value considering his starting price with the bookmakers was around 2.00.

As Paire's projected hold was also very low at 64.4% (over 11% below the ATP clay average) there was massive value opposing his serve in this match – not only was his pre-match price flawed, but also his projected hold was much lower than average.

This is a prime example of using projected hold models to our advantage to establish both pre-match and in-play value. In this case, both were in our favour.

Paire played 18 service games in the match. He gave Nishikori 19 break points, of which 8 were converted by the Japanese player. The ratio of 1.06 break points per game was significantly higher than the current ATP clay mean of 0.59 break points per game, and Paire actually held his serve 55.6% of the time, even lower than our projected hold model indicated. This was about 20% below the ATP clay average and indicates what superb value this approach was – and how much money we would have made opposing every Paire service game (before the match was a foregone conclusion).

Getting the information you need

To identify pre-match value looking at projected holds, you can get the information you need by signing up for the TennisRatings Daily Spreadsheet via **www.tennisratings.co.uk**. It is not essential that you do this as you could calculate this information yourself by working through the array of statistics on the internet, paying particular attention to the surface stats in the last year and also the last three months.

Identifying value

If a player holds more and breaks more than their opponent but is priced as underdog, without obvious extenuating circumstances as to why, then we have identified the underdog should in fact be favourite and we can trade on the basis that the player is value. Alternatively, if a player holds and breaks slightly less than their opponent, but their opponent is very short odds (particularly under 1.40 pre-match), then we can also assume that the underdog is a good value proposition because the projected holds are close and the price does not reflect that.

Pre-match Lay to In-Play Back

SHORT-PRICED FAVOURITES

A *PRE-MATCH LAY TO IN-PLAY BACK* CAN BE A GREAT way of opposing short priced players. As the name suggests, we lay a very short priced player pre-match, with a view to backing them at a higher price later on during the match.

Clearly at this point our view – just looking for a short-priced player and hoping their price will increase during the match – would be a subjective, or qualitative, assessment of the player's chances.

I'm not particularly a fan of qualitative assessments and always look for quantitative solutions. Therefore, having built my effective projected hold model primarily for in-play trading, one of the many advantages of it is that it can indicate which favourites are priced far too short for the match.

It's not uncommon for a big name to be priced below 1.20 pre-match, and even well below 1.10. A lot of the time this is very justified – Rafael Nadal on clay, for example, hardly ever loses to non-elite opponents. However, there are many occasions where it's not so justified – Andy Murray on clay, as we've discussed already, is a prime example.

In the 2013 clay season, Murray played six matches. He was pre-match favourite in all those six matches despite having atrocious clay stats for a player of his rank. In five of the six matches, he started at a price below 1.50. The only straightforward victory he had was against Edouard Roger-Vasselin (1.09 SP) and in the four other matches his price increased a great deal – he lost the first set against Stanislas Wawrinka, Gilles Simon and Marcel Granollers, all of whom were ranked below the top 15 at the time. Against Florian Mayer, Murray won both sets on a tiebreak, but having started at 1.13 SP, his price drifted until he took the tiebreak.

If we had laid-to-back Murray pre-match in the five matches he was priced below 1.45, we would have made a significant profit in four of the five matches, because his opening price was far too low.

There are other players that are overrated, particularly on certain surfaces that they may not be that comfortable on. The market tends to price a player on reputation fairly often, so these players can be way too short in the pre-match markets.

This is an area where it really pays to do your research and check a player's recent win-loss record on a surface, and also their serve and return statistics on that surface. If a player has a very mediocre record on the surface, and the serve and return statistics for both players are reasonably close (e.g. within 5% of each), then we can consider the short priced favourite as too short in the betting.

PRICES TO LOOK FOR

Regarding the prices at which I look to perform this trade, personally I will not lay a player pre-match with a view to backing them later unless they are priced below 1.40. Ideally they will be much shorter, below 1.20, reducing the potential liability further.

At what point we back the player later on in the set, if the trade is going in our favour, is purely down to your own tolerance of risk. Personally if the favourite goes a break down and therefore I have a decent profit I will at least clear my liability from laying the favourite. Depending on how bad the value was on the favourite pre-match I may leave all my profit on the underdog for the set, or split it equally.

If I clear my pre-match liability when the underdog goes a break up, obviously if the favourite goes on and loses the set I lose some potential profit due to backing the favourite at a lower price at a break down compared to the price I could get if I let the pre-match lay run until the end of the set. But I've taken less risk, which is always important to me. There's no shame in protecting your trading bank.

Backing the Favourite When Losing

AFAVOURITE TACTIC OF NOVICE TENNIS TRADERS IS to *lay the underdog when leading*, or *back the favourite when losing*. Effectively they are the same thing. You see a lot of people advocating this trade on Twitter – I've noticed it's a particular favourite of cricket traders making their way over to the tennis markets.

The thought process is that the favourite was a favourite pre-match because the market thought they were the better player before the match started and surely they'll come through in the end. I hate to ruin anyone's perceptions but to be brutally honest, this is a load of rubbish.

Favourites do lose and they lose on more than the odd occasion. Furthermore, as we will see later in the 'At the end of the first set' section, my statistics prove that the market support for this entry point means that often you are backing the favourite at an artificially low price, sometimes up to 20 ticks below the true market value.

I'm not saying this isn't ever a viable entry point, but you need to consider a few things before making this entry:

* Does the favourite have a good record of coming back either from break deficits or from set deficits?

* Does the underdog have a history of choking in pressure situations such as when on the verge of a big win or when serving for the match?

* What is the biggest win that the underdog has achieved in their career or in the last year? If the favourite is of a significantly higher level than that, perhaps this could still be a viable trade.

* Does the favourite have a good record of beating much lower ranked players?

* Is the underdog a bad server or does the favourite have a strong return game? If either (or preferably both of these) are applicable then we may be able to enter at this point. We may not get (or need to get) the result of the favourite winning the match but if the favourite comes back and gets a break back, we can still exit the trade profitably.

* Does the favourite have a high level of motivation to win this match? Player motivation tends to be highest in Grand Slams and Masters (1000) events (the women's equivalent of these is WTA Premier events) as there is more money and ranking points on offer. Therefore if a favourite is losing to an underdog in a low-profile 250/WTA International event we need to be very wary of their motivation. This can especially be the case in the more exotic locations, where a few days on the beach or by the pool can be considered much more of a priority by some top players.

Bearing in mind a heavy pre-match favourite may still be trading odds-on even after losing the first set, backing them has a big risk attached to it because their price still can rise much more than it can fall. I would strongly recommend at least a few of the above conditions are met before you make this trade.

Laying Bad Servers

ONE TYPE OF TRADE THAT I LIKE IS *OPPOSING THE very bad servers*. My projected hold model enables me to identify these easily. A player that has a projected hold of below 64% (ATP) or below 50% (WTA) is a prime candidate for this trade and can be laid on pretty much all their service games.

As I mentioned previously, the market is still fairly unaware of this and tends to be far too orientated to starting price, which is then deviated by the current score.

Looking at the WTA stats for matches over the last year, I think the lowest projected hold I've ever seen was Rus against Errani in the first round of the French Open in 2013. It was 27% for Rus. She'd only held around 35% of her service games in the last three months and Errani's return game is one of the best on the WTA tour. Considering Serena Williams holds around 85% of the time on clay it shows the huge difference between the top and the bottom of the tour.

Anyone with any experience of tennis trading will know that even on the WTA tour the market will shorten by fewer ticks when the serve is held than it will rise when serve is broken. As I mentioned previously, it's very difficult to say exactly what the risk/reward ratio is in this situation as it varies so much based on the scoreline, but my research shows that the range 61-62% for service holds on the WTA is generally about right. So, for example, if the market shortens a player by around 15 ticks for a hold then it will lengthen a player 25 ticks for a break. (15/25 = 60%). It's highly situational though.

I would generally apply my projected hold analysis in the following way when laying the server:

ATP:

* **64-74% projected hold** – lay the player when serving a break up and exit the trade at the end of the set if the opponent does not break back.

* **Under 64% projected hold** – lay the player when serving when the match is on serve and when they are leading by a break. If you lay the player when the match is on serve you need to exit the trade at the end of the service game regardless of whether the market moved in your favour with a break, or against you with a hold. When they are leading by a break you can leave the trade until the end of the set – you're waiting to see if the break-back occurs. In this situation you would be looking to clear liability or hedge with profit to some extent if the match went back on serve (the trade went your way) or hedge for a loss if the player served out the set (the trade went against you).

WTA:

* **50-60% projected hold** – lay the player when serving a break up and exit the trade at the end of the set if the opponent does not break back.

* **Under 50% projected hold** – lay the player when serving when the match is on serve and when they are leading by a break. If you lay the player when the match is on serve you need to exit the trade at the end of the service game regardless of whether the market moved in your favour with a break, or against you with a hold. When they are leading by a break you can leave the trade until the end of the set – you're waiting to see if the break-back occurs. In this situation you would be looking to clear liability or hedge with profit to some extent if the match went back on serve (the trade went your way) or hedge for a loss if the player served out the set (the trade went against you).

* However, I would take into account the current prices before executing these trades. Generally I will only trade matches in this way where the favourite is priced at 1.40 or higher. Furthermore, I will generally only oppose the bad server if my projected hold model does not consider the player value.

I will give two examples from the women's French Open second round matches on 30 May 2013.

Example 1: Kristina Mladenovic v Sam Stosur

Mladenovic had a projected hold of 52.1% and Stosur had a projected hold of 71.1%. My model and other adjustments perceived that the starting price of 1.25 on Stosur was pretty much spot-on. As Mladenovic has a projected hold of 52.1%, we should be getting some advantage if we laid her when a break up (that never actually happened, but it doesn't detract from the example) because it's significantly below the WTA average for service holds. Of course, we must slightly temper that approach with realising that market support on Stosur – as she started as a high-profile heavy favourite – will probably mean her in-play price will be artificially low.

Example 2: Alize Cornet v Silvia Soler-Espinosa

This match was a completely different proposition. Soler-Espinosa in this match and Mladenovic in the first example had a very similar projected hold – Soler-Espinosa's was 51.8%. Cornet's was 59.0%. However, my model and other adjustments considered Soler-Espinosa value based on her pre-match starting price (3.05), which I felt should be around 2.60. Therefore, I would be far less willing to oppose Soler-Espinosa, even though she has a low projected hold, in the knowledge that my model indicated that her starting price was too high. If my model was correct, and it's the lifeblood of my trading, then my value on laying her with a low projected hold would be eroded by the incorrect starting price.

Women's and men's games

There is a widespread perception that female players are terrible at holding serve. I'm as guilty as anybody in using the term *WTA match* to describe a match with many breaks. There are some terrible servers and knowledge of these can be highly advantageous. However, there are some very good servers who hold serve consistently over 70% of the time. You would not want to oppose these players unless they are facing a player who breaks with extreme regularity (over 50% of the time) compared to the averages.

On the flip side, I think that a lot of people appear to think it's a given that a man holds serve. Believe it or not, there are some men (and not necessarily the lower level players either) that hold around 70% or less.

Gilles Simon is currently ranked 18th in the world (and has been as high as 6th) and in 14 clay matches in 2013 held serve just 70.5% of the time – which is over 5% below the ATP average. He does break 35% of the time in those matches, however – perhaps indicating why he is one of my favourite players to trade in this manner.

The Vesnina Trade

THIS IS ONE OF MY FAVOURITE TRADES AND WORKS especially well in the WTA. I have used it a great deal but didn't have a name for it until Elena Vesnina earned me a significant amount of money from it against Monica Niculescu in April 2013, coming back twice from double break deficits in the first and second sets. I could have also named it after Li Na, for her propensity to throw away dominant leads in sets.

The premise of this trade is that you *lay a bad server that is a double break up in either the first or second set of the match*, as soon as the double break has been obtained.

HOW THE TRADE WORKS

The reason why I like the trade so much is that the risk is incredibly minimal. If you lay a player at a scoreline like 4-0 up in a set the market perceives it's almost a given that the player will win the set. Only if the player wins the set 6-0 do you have more than the tiniest of losses. Even if the scoreline goes from 4-0 to 6-2, you often find that you incur no more than a 5 tick loss, and sometimes you may even gain a small profit if the player losing 4-0 shows themselves to be competitive for the rest of the set.

Of course, winning the set is not easy from 4-0 down. However, getting a break back is much easier. Many players tend to take their foot off the gas when leading by a double break in a set, getting a little complacent. Naturally, some players when losing consider the double break down situation a lost cause but these tend to be the same players that aren't good when a set down either, so we can work out who these players are fairly easily and avoid them with this trade.

What I tend to do is clear my liability when one break back is obtained. So I will have £0 profit/loss on the player leading (now by a single break) and all my profit on the player a break down. If they then hold serve I might drip a little profit over to the player leading as the price has moved further in my favour, depending on my stats. If the double break back is lost, and the set goes back on serve, we are in for a huge result as we can then equalise our significant profit across both players.

EXAMPLE FROM KVITOVA VERSUS BECK

A superb example of this was the match in Stuttgart in April 2013 between Petra Kvitova and Annika Beck. I remember this match because it was my record for a single break back in this trade: 38 ticks.

Kvitova started at around 1.25 and found herself a double break down at 4-1, on Beck's serve in the first set. I can't remember the exact prices, but she would have not been too far off 2.00 at this point.

Winning this match would be by far Beck's biggest win in tennis. Not only that – she also has a very weak serve. With Kvitova being above average on return stats, it was clear that unless something very unlikely happened, Kvitova would be able to create a lot of pressure on Beck's serve. Indeed, Kvitova had a break point on Beck's serve in the previous service game.

You may recall earlier I said to be wary of backing favourites when losing. That still stands, but with so much sting taken out of the price, compared to the starting price, I had little to lose. Furthermore, with the market support clearly going to be on the big name player, Kvitova, should she get back into this match I was going to be in a great situation.

Therefore I backed Kvitova at around evens and she then broke Beck for *2-4. Now she only trailed by a single break – and I cleared my liability by laying at 38 ticks below my back price. All my profit was now on Kvitova and I was prepared to leave it like that until either she lost the set (I would still be in profit if that happened) or she got the set back on serve. And that was exactly what happened. She held and then broke Beck again to get the scores level at 4-4. With momentum clearly in Kvitova's favour and the scoreboard level, Kvitova's price decreased to around the starting price and I levelled my profit by laying at around 1.30.

I managed to make a huge profit, incurring very little risk. If Kvitova lost the set, my loss would have been minimal compared to the potential profit available even if she got just a single break back.

DATA ANALYSIS

You might be reading this thinking that players hardly ever come back from a double break down. I decided to sample months of data and the following statistics illustrate that they do:

* When a bad server (under 74% projected hold) was a double break up in the ATP they were broken back at least once 26.7% of the time. The double break was lost 6.8% of the time.

* When a bad server (under 60% projected hold) was a double break up in the WTA they were broken back at least once 49.8% of the time. The double break was lost 14.8% of the time.

From these statistics, we can see that in the WTA we make a profit almost half the time, and when we do our profit is significantly higher than the minimal risk we incur. Even in the ATP, as long as our potential profit is about four times higher than our minimal risk (it usually is), we can also use this strategy profitably.

REDUCING AN AVERAGE LAY POSITION

Another way we can use this trade is to reduce our average lay position in an attempt to trade out of a bad position. The hypothetical example below illustrates this.

We decide to lay a bad server at *2-0 at 1.50
for £100 stake (£50 liability).

Unfortunately the trade goes against us and we find ourselves in a bad spot at *4-0 down with the player trading now at 1.20.

If we now lay the same player again at 1.20 for £100 stake we add £20 liability to our position.

At this point our liability is £70 and our potential profit is £200. If we divide £70 by £200 we get 0.35 – so our average lay price is now 1.35 instead of the 1.50 we originally laid at.

So – as long as the player now trades at 1.35 or higher we can eradicate our loss, should we decide to do so – instead of the 1.50 that we had to get back up to previously. A break back at this point would definitely push the price over 1.35, and our position back into profit.

I will discuss the **averaging down** technique more in the chapter Dealing With Losing Positions.

Pressure Situations

IN TENNIS, THERE ARE A NUMBER OF PRESSURE POINTS that a player must negotiate to win a match. I will look at a couple of these now:

* Serving for the set.

* Serving to stay in the set.

1. SERVING FOR THE SET

Clearly, serving for the set (with a single break advantage) is going to be a pressure situation. The phrase *choking* is often used to describe a player's failure to hold their serve when in this key situation. Whilst that term is slightly derogatory, it accurately summarises the situation in most cases. The player has let the pressure get to them at a critical point in the match.

On that basis, it would be reasonable to think that laying the server in these situations would be a lucrative entry point. However, for several reasons, I dislike this entry point in most cases.

Why I dislike this entry

Firstly, because it's to win a set – a key part of the match – the downside regarding the amount of ticks lost if the server holds is significantly higher than opposing the server in a normal service game. Whilst it's true that previous events in the set have caused some drop of the starting price, this is still going to be a significant loss if the player holds.

Considering the normal gain if a break is achieved when a player is serving for the set is barely, if any, bigger than a break back at a normal time, you will want to ensure that if you are laying a player in this situation they have a proven track record for choking and also a very low projected hold percentage.

Secondly, my statistics show that there is no significant likelihood that the average bad server holds their serve any less than they would normally be expected to. There is a phenomenon in life where people generally remember more significant incidents than more minor ones, and I think this situation falls into that category. People naturally are going to remember a player failing to serve out a set more than a player getting broken at *2-1 up as it's a higher profile situation. Therefore people think this happens more due to it being a more significant event.

Average service games compared to games serving for the set

In the sample that I carried out, I surveyed all service games for players with a projected hold below 74% in the ATP. The mean projected hold was 67.2%, but these players held their serve when serving for the set on 66.7% of occasions. So there was barely any difference whatsoever (and certainly not a statistically significant difference) between an average service game and serving to win the set.

The situation was far worse for the women with a projected hold below 60%. A widely held perception is that many female players struggle mentally in pressure situations but the statistics fail to back that up. In fact, the opposite was found to be the case. The mean projected hold was 56.6%, but these players held their serve when serving for the set 64.6% of the time.

This is very interesting because not only is the 64.6% above the 63.6% mean for WTA service holds across all surfaces, it's above the 61-62% risk/reward ratio I mentioned previously. When you add the fact that the tick gain for this situation is higher than a normal service game too, it appears that backing generally bad serving women when serving for the set almost certainly has a positive expectation. This is fantastic when you consider that the vast majority of the market will be thinking the opposite.

2. SERVING TO STAY IN THE SET

As with serving for a set, *serving to stay in the set* is another pressure situation that a player often faces in a match. Please note here that I'm taking about when the set is currently on serve, so in this situation the scoreline would be either *4-5 or *5-6. So if the server lost the game, he or she would lose the set.

This situation is slightly lower profile for most fans, pundits and traders than serving for a set, although effectively the pressure is likely to be the same on the player serving. They will be acutely aware that a failure to hold this service game will cost them the set and sometimes the match.

As with laying the server when serving for the set, initially it would appear that this would be a viable entry point. However, as we saw previously, I disproved that theory. I will again use statistics to assess whether the same is true laying the server when serving to stay in the set.

Analysing the situation

First of all, it's important to mention that the tick loss you would incur if you laid the server and they then held serve when serving to stay in the set would almost always be less than if you had laid the server when they were serving to win the set and they held their serve. That is because if the server holds their serve when serving to stay in the set, the set will still be on serve after the service game, as opposed to being finished if the server held when serving for the set. However, the tick gain for a break will often be bigger because if the player fails to serve out the set, it's the end of the set. So on that basis it's much more promising than laying a player serving to win the set – the loss you are risking is less and the potential gain is greater.

Interestingly, the statistics also gave me insight that this was a much more viable entry point.

We saw earlier that in the ATP in my sample of bad servers, the mean projected hold was 67.2% – when serving for the set the player held on 66.7% of occasions. That was almost the same as the mean and showed no edge. However, when serving to stay in the set we did get a small edge.

This time the server only held on average 62.9% of the time – a 4.3% decrease from the mean.

This is fascinating because effectively the pressure should be very similar and led me to wonder why there was lower success for a player serving to stay in the set than serving for the set. I have no definitive answer for that, but the only thing I can think of is that the player serving for the set is often the 'better player' because they are in the lead by a break in the set, and hence would be more likely to succeed more often in serving the game out to win the set.

This disparity was also apparent in the WTA. We saw previously the mean projected hold was 56.6% for the bad servers sampled when serving for the set. We also saw that the player serving for the set held 64.6% of the time (above the 63.6% WTA mean across all surfaces) – higher than average and way higher than the average for the bad servers sampled.

However, when serving to stay in the set, things were different. This time the bad servers held much less frequently, on 54.9% of occasions. This was 1.4% below the mean for the bad servers sampled and a huge 9.5% below the WTA mean across all surfaces.

Therefore we can start to draw conclusions about this strategy. Not only do servers serving to stay in the set at *4-5 or *5-6 hold serve less often than in the average ATP/WTA service game, the potential tick gain should be bigger and the tick loss should be smaller. It is clear that laying the server when serving to stay in the set would be much more advantageous than laying the server when serving for the set.

Backing The Server

SOME PEOPLE LIKE THIS TRADE, BUT IT'S DEFINITELY not a personal favourite of mine. It revolves around *backing a good server* when serving and is based on the premise that you get likely, small profits, as opposed to less likely, bigger profits that you get from laying a server.

However, this strategy is not viable for me for several reasons.

WHY I DO NOT FAVOUR THIS STRATEGY

Firstly, I don't like the risk/reward ratio. Surely it is better to have some small losses and big gains than small gains and bigger losses, even though the gains are more frequent in this strategy? Depending on the set and the stage of the set, a break of serve can cost you well in excess of 70 ticks – why would you want to expose yourself to that level of risk?

Secondly, the market is much more aware of the *big servers* that this method requires than the bad servers that laying bad servers needs. Therefore, the tick gain for a service hold would be smaller than in a match between two lower profile players.

For example, a typical low-profile match featuring *bad player vs bad player* tends to have below average service holds because those players tend to have stronger return games than service games. Most people betting on tennis don't trade using statistics, so it will be less well known in the market that the projected holds for a low-profile match or player will be low than it is that projected holds for a high-profile big server will be high. Simply, there is better value in seeking out the low-profile matches, rather than backing big servers.

Example from Kubot versus Teixeira

An example of this is the Lukasz Kubot v Maxime Teixeira match in the 1st round of the French Open on 28 May 2013. Kubot is an ATP journeyman with a pretty poor record on clay. Teixeira plays most of his tennis on the lower level Challenger and ITF tours and qualified for this match. Kubot started at 1.41 for this match and that was perhaps a little generous based on the projected holds.

Kubot on clay in ATP matches held serve 69.5% of the time from 12 matches (in my sample from 28 May 2012 to 28 May 2013). This is well below the ATP mean clay hold percentage of 75.9% – yet he is not regarded as a true bad server. Teixeira has little ATP experience, but looking at his Challenger tour record and adjusting it accordingly, it would give him an average ATP hold of 57.2%. Again, very low. He may not necessarily be a bad server (I've never actually seen him play!) but because his game is generally so limited at the highest level he will struggle to hold serve.

Here the final projected hold percentages worked out to be 70.1% for Kubot and 55.9% for Teixeira. Therefore we have found a match with low projected holds, simply because of the low quality of the two players, which may fly under most people's radars.

In the match, there were 42 service games, 21 for each player. Kubot had 21 break points (well above the average of 0.59 break points per game for clay) and broke 8 times in the 21 Teixeira service games (61.9% hold for Teixeira – so my pre-match maths was pretty solid).

However, despite being favourite, Kubot himself gave 11 break point chances to Teixeira (a ratio of 0.52 break points per game, which is not far from the ATP mean and is still a good stat considering Kubot started 1.4 favourite) and Teixeira took 6 of those. That meant Kubot held 71.0% of his service games, almost exactly the same as his projected hold of 70.1%. Effectively I managed to pick a match where projected holds were low, but didn't feature a notorious bad server, such as Volandri, Kavcic or Kamke, for example.

And that, in essence, is the exact problem of backing a good server when serving. The good servers are notorious.

NOTORIETY OF GOOD SERVERS

Ask any tennis fan who a good server is and the same names crop up. Isner. Raonic. Anderson. Querrey. Janowicz. Karlovic. Backing these players when serving would give no edge because even someone with basic tennis knowledge knows that these players are more likely to hold serve than Volandri, Kavcic or Kamke. So clearly the market will know too.

For the *backing the server* strategy to have any chance of working – if you aren't put off completely by the poor risk/reward ratio! – you will need to find players who have a high projected hold percentage but aren't known big servers. This could possibly be someone who has a reasonably solid serve (perhaps several percent above the ATP mean) but is playing someone with an extremely limited return game (especially on a given surface).

For example, Denis Istomin on clay has, in my opinion, exactly such a weak return game. He broke serve a mere 12% of the time in his 13 clay matches in 2013, well below the ATP mean of 24.1%. Other players with low break percentages on clay from a reasonable sample in 2013 include Bernard Tomic, Jurgen Melzer, Andrey Kuznetsov, Philipp Kohlschreiber and Martin Alund. Also Igor Sijsling broke serve just 16% of the time across all surfaces from his 20 matches in 2013. Backing solid but not notoriously strong servers against poor returners like these could be a possible area to look at for this strategy.

Generally, I much prefer backing good servers in-game when losing in that game. I will examine that topic further in the section In-Game Trades: 1. Backing The Good Server.

Tiebreak Trading

TIEBREAKS ARE A VERY VOLATILE PERIOD FOR IN-play trading. For those who are unaware, a tiebreak is played when a set reaches 6 games each. The first to 7 points wins the tiebreak and the set, although the player must win by 2 clear points. The first player to serve does so for one point, and then the serve rotates every two points. It usually takes roughly 10-15 points for the winner of the set to be decided and consequently there are heavy swings when a player wins a point, particularly when a player wins a point on the opponent's serve.

If a player starts the match at 1.25, they might be about 1.35 at the time of a tiebreak in the first set. If they win the tiebreak, their price will probably be under 1.10, but if they were to lose it, it would be likely to be around 2.00. Therefore, in a short space of time, a huge odds swing is guaranteed one way or the other.

I personally trade tiebreaks only when I have a live video stream and I also trade them with significantly reduced stakes due to the volatility.

There is, to some extent, a degree of luck and randomness in tiebreaks. Although there's definitely an element of skill and mental strength too – some players with consistently good tiebreak records like John Isner prove that. Incredibly, Robin Haase once lost 17 tiebreaks in a row, so clearly he was not strong in the key points.

Big servers tend to have a little bit more success in tiebreaks, although it's not a given that this is the case. Many pundits often are highly unsurprised when the likes of Ivo Karlovic win a tiebreak, but actually his career tiebreak record at the time of writing is a non-spectacular 199-185 (52% win-rate). Probably the main reason why a big server is generally slightly more successful in tiebreaks is because they have more practice – due to their serving quality and generally mediocre return game they have a higher chance of getting to tiebreaks than the average player.

MY STRATEGY IN TIEBREAKS

What I look to do in tiebreaks is to try and oppose players who have a generally low pre-match projected hold percentage for all service games, as determined by my analysis. The price will move hugely against the player that loses a service point in a tiebreak, so we can make a lot of ticks if a player with a low projected hold loses a service point in a tiebreak.

If we look at some stats, you can start to get an idea of the maths behind this.

In the ATP, across all surfaces, the current mean for service points won is 63.1%, but the average service hold is higher at 78.2%. So if we consider laying players on serve in tiebreaks with a projected hold of under 64% (very bad server category) then their average points won on serve should be around the 51-55% mark.

Let's assume that a player has a 64% projected hold and we are generous and assign them 55% success for winning points on their serve.

The likelihood of that player winning two straight points on their serve in a tiebreak – and us losing the trade – is a mere 30.25% (55%*55%). For the receiver to win both points the likelihood is slightly lower, at 20.25% (45%*45%). Therefore, the likelihood for both players to win a point each on a low projected hold player's tiebreak mini-service game is 49.50% ((55%*45%)+(45%*55%)). That too would guarantee us a profit after the mini service game as we gain more ticks for the receiver winning one point than we would lose for the server winning one point.

So mathematically in this situation we have a 69.75% of making a profit (20.25% + 49.50%). Unfortunately the 30.25% chance of the receiver losing both points would represent a significant loss, although that would be dwarfed by the potential profit should the 20.25% chance of the receiver winning both points happen. There's very little you can do about avoiding the chance of the server winning both points – it happens. But that's the thing with trading tiebreaks – if you want to trade them you need to accept the fact that there is a chance of losing a high percentage of your stake.

It's also vital to realise that tiebreaks are very quick. New regulations mean that the server has 25 seconds (20 seconds in a Grand Slam) from the end of the previous point to start the next point. You will need to be very quick to ensure your trades get matches. This is a very pressurised time in tennis trading.

OTHER WAYS TO TRADE TIEBREAKS

There is one very low-risk method of trading tiebreaks. If a player is 6-2 or 6-3 up in a tiebreak, the market generally assumes that the tiebreak is as good as over. If you lay a player leading by this score (or of course back the player losing by that score), the market barely moves when the tiebreak is won (especially from 6-2). In fact, if you often wait for a minute or so after the set for the market to correct itself then you sometimes even find you can trade out with a tick or two profit!

If the player you have laid loses the next point or two and the score gets to perhaps 6-4, then you can exit with a decent profit (perhaps at that point you can clear your liability and keep the profit riding on the player 6-4 down). Players do lose tiebreaks from 6-2 and 6-3 up, so for such low risk this is a great trade.

Another way of trading it is to lay at the same entry point (6-2 or 6-3) and keep the trade in place until the end of the tiebreak. That way you get the gigantic tick gain if your player stages an unlikely comeback and wins the tiebreak, but even if the player you backed loses the tiebreak by a score like 7-5 or 8-6 you should make some profit as the price at that point will be higher than your lay price as the tiebreak was won less dominantly than when you laid the leader.

In-Game Trades

T HE NEXT THREE SECTIONS LOOK AT TRADES YOU can make during individual games.

1. BACKING THE GOOD SERVER

As I previously mentioned, I'm not a fan of backing good servers – especially notoriously good servers in their service games – due to the poor risk/reward ratio. However, one way that we can reduce the risk is to *back players with a high projected hold* (again – especially those players who aren't known good servers) *when losing in their service games*.

Because we are backing the server when losing in their service game, the price we back the player at is higher than at a game score of 0-0. Therefore this will reduce our tick loss should the server lose their service game. Not only this, but our potential tick gain is greater because we are backing them at a better price than at the start of the service game.

The problem of liquidity

Before this trading strategy begins to sound too good to be true, I need to point out something pretty vital. In-game liquidity isn't the best. Personally, I only trade in-game on live streamed matches with £100,000 or more matched in the market before the match starts.

For non-live matches, it's possible to work out the in-game score in advance of a live score website by just watching the markets move but I would definitely not recommend this for a beginner. With liquidity not being the best, it's often difficult to get large trades matched too, so this type of trading strategy isn't very scalable for non-live matches.

To cope with illiquid markets, you will need to offer prices. In this process, you are looking to create prices, rather than simply taking them, and this requires more than a basic level of experience. This also may mean that you aren't getting such good value as you would in a liquid market, which would have a one tick difference between the back and lay prices. The more experienced you get in the markets, the easier you will find this as you will begin to be able to anticipate the tick movement per point depending on the match state. To give a very general example, if a player is something like 1.52 to back and 1.57 to lay immediately following a point, if you offer 1.54 or 1.55 either way you will have a very good chance of being matched.

You need to try and get the trade offered immediately after a point is finished because, as with tiebreaks, it's vital to be very quick to get your trades matched. As soon as the server throws the ball in the air on the Betfair video, if my entry trade isn't matched, I cancel it. With the new legislation allowing just 20-25 seconds per point, you need to be very quick, especially considering Betfair have the five-second delay for trades to be placed. This type of quick trading isn't for everyone.

Now that's out of the way, I want to discuss the various entry points for this strategy.

Entry points

ATP analysis

When I first decided to look at this trading strategy, I backtested various scenarios to see which entry points were more lucrative than others and achieved some pretty interesting results.

To start with, I ruled out any score that meant the server was down by one point (e.g. 0-15, 15-30, 30-40 or 40-A) because the tick loss will still be very heavy should the server be broken.

So that narrowed down the sample to 0-30, 0-40, or 15-40 as potential entry points. As I am a fairly risk-averse trader, I wanted to assess how my selected players would fare winning both the next point and the next two points. I didn't want to leave winning trades any longer than that.

In the ATP, the average player across all surfaces wins 63.1% of service points (holding 78.2% of the time). I looked at players with a projected hold of over 81% (so at least 2.8% above the ATP mean).

At 0-30, players with a projected hold of over 81% won the next point 66.7% of the time, well above those averages. They won the next two points on 46.7% of occasions (6.9% above the all surfaces average of 39.8% (63.1%*63.1%)) so clearly this would be a very viable entry point as a big server wins significantly more points at this scoreline than would be expected of an average player.

However, at 0-40, the situation was vastly different. This was not a good entry point whatsoever. My results show that even strong servers struggle at this point – perhaps players consider that game to be a foregone conclusion by that point. In my sample of strong servers, they only won the next point 48.8% of the time – well below the average for even the weakest of servers on any normal points. The stats for winning the next two points were also not fantastic – a success rate of 33.3%, again below average. So whilst the risk is incredibly low backing a server at 0-40, the reward is much less likely to happen than at 0-30.

Finally, I examined the stats for the 15-40 entry point. This actually was the best entry point of the three sampled. The server won the next service points 69.5% of the time, which is 6.4% above the fair average. Furthermore, the server won the next two points a huge 53.7% of the time. This is fantastic because if we enter at 15-40 with our exit points either at a break of serve or hedging in some way at 40-40, this means we are slightly more likely to win our trade than lose it. There is also no doubt that our tick profit will be greater going from 15-40 to 40-40 than our loss would be from 15-40 to service break so our winning trades will also have more profit than the losses our losing trades incur.

WTA analysis

I also did the same sample for the WTA – looking at players who had projected holds over 67%. Remarkably, the results were almost parallel to the ATP.

As with the ATP, 0-40 was by far the worst entry point. The average WTA player wins 55.8% of their service points but in this sample women with high projected holds won just 55.0% of the time to take it to 15-40 – slightly below WTA average. However, when getting the next point to 15-40, the women often took the next point as well. Going from 0-40 to 30-40 occurred 38.1% of the time – above the 31.1% expectancy. So this indicates that 15-40 would be a viable entry point.

This was confirmed in emphatic style as in the sample the high projected hold women won the next point from 15-40 to 30-40 64.6% of the time (8.8% above the WTA mean) and 37.5% won the next two points to take it to 40-40 (6.4% above the 31.1% expectancy). Clearly this is a very good entry point.

That can also be said for the 0-30 entry point where 60.8% of women with high projected holds won the next point to 15-30 in my sample – 5.0% above WTA mean. Not only this, they were very successful winning the next point as well, to 30-30. This occurred on 42.9% of occasions – a huge 11.8% above average. So the statistics found this to be an excellent entry point as well.

Summary

It can therefore be said that 0-30 and 15-40 are excellent entry points to back players with high projected holds for both the ATP and WTA. These entry points have much less risk than backing these players at 0-0 in the game and they produce significant rewards when they are successful.

2. OPPOSING THE BAD SERVER

In a similar vein, I assessed in-game entry points with a view to *opposing those with low projected holds when leading in their service games*. Due to the average lower tick loss discussed previously, the risk of laying the server before the game starts isn't nearly as high as backing a server before it. However, reducing that risk further can never be a bad thing.

Opposing a bad server if they are leading in their service game achieves this purpose, as the tick loss that you would get should you lay a bad server pre-service game will be reduced if we lay them when they are winning that service game, as the price will have moved prior to our entry point.

Entry points

The lower risk of this setup means I am able to be more liberal with my entry points and I am quite willing to look at situations where the bad server is one point ahead.

ATP data

For the ATP, I looked at the following entry points:

30-0, 40-0, 30-15, 40-15, 40-30 and A-40. (My analysis lead me to omit 15-0, as this did not offer such a good setup.)

As I noted previously, the average ATP receiver wins 36.9% of points and consequently they win the next two return points 13.6% of the time (36.9%*36.9%). In this sample, I looked at players with under a 70% projected hold only.

The results are shown in the table below:

Score	% of times receiver won next point	% of times receiver won next two points
30-0	36.2% (-0.7% below average)	12.8% (-0.8% below average)
40-0	26.1% (-10.8%)	13.6% (exactly average)
30-15	40.9% (+4.0%)	16.2% (+2.6%)
40-15	40.0% (+3.1%)	17.2% (+3.6%)
40-30	41.3% (+4.4%)	19.6% (+6.0%)
A-40	38.8% (+1.9%)	13.4% (-0.2%)

When I looked at this data, two things stared me in the face.

Firstly, the lack of success at the 40-0 entry point, which immediately led me to draw parallels to the poor statistics for backing players with a high projected hold at 0-40 in the previous chapter. It makes me believe even more that many tennis players believe that when they are losing 0-40 in a game it is a foregone conclusion and they have less motivation at this scoreline than at other points.

The second thing I noticed is the disparity in success between scorelines where the receiver hadn't won a point and when they had. It appears from these statistics that the receiver winning at least a point on their opponent's serve gives them huge encouragement and this look at their opponent's service game ensures that they put maximum effort in for that service game.

Clearly we can disregard 30-0 and 40-0 as entry points for laying players with a low projected hold from these statistics. However, laying these players at 30-15, 40-15 and 40-30 especially provides us with a decent edge that we should be able to exploit.

WTA sample

Building on what I learned in the ATP sample, I focused on the points where the receiver had won at least one point in my similar WTA sample, namely the 30-15, 40-15, 40-30 and A-40 scorelines.

As I noted in the previous chapter, the average WTA player wins 55.8% of service points (hence the average receiver wins 44.2% of points) and consequently the average receiver wins the next point 19.5% of the time (44.2%*44.2%).

The table below shows the results of the WTA sample:

Score	% of times receiver won next point	% of times receiver won next two points
30-15	46.5% (+2.3%)	24.8% (+5.3%)
40-15	41.5% (-2.7%)	22.9% (+3.4%)
40-30	52.3% (+8.1%)	20.9% (+1.1%)
A-40	49.1% (+4.9%)	27.3% (+7.8%)

As we can see, all entry points except the 40-15 entry point (interestingly the only entry point I sampled with a two point lead in the game) provided above average results. This definitely backs up the theory that the more success a player has previously in the service game (notwithstanding the fact they are still losing it), the more success they are likely to enjoy for the rest of it.

In particular, if we oppose a WTA server with a low projected hold at 40-30 and A-40, we can expect an above average level of success to get the game back on level terms at 40-40 and longer-term trades of the next two points work well from 30-15 and A-40.

3. BREAK POINTS

Break points can be another possible entry point for in-game trading. Obviously, some players are better than others at break points, either saving or converting them. Amongst other qualities needed to be good at saving break points is mental strength, which some players have much more of than others.

In April 2013, I analysed the top 100 ATP and WTA players to assess which players were the best and worst at saving break points.

Interestingly, the average percentage of break points saved in the ATP was 59.9%, but the average server in the sample won 62.7% of points, so the average break point was 2.8% more likely to be won by the receiver than any normal point.

This was almost the same in the WTA. Here, 56.1% of points were won on serve but only 53.8% of break points were saved, so the average break point was 2.3% more likely to be won by the receiver than any normal point.

In search of the best break point savers

So, clearly, if a player saves more break points than normal points, they can be considered to have strong mental strength in this situation. In my opinion, it's vital to compare break point save percentages to service won percentages to get this score, as opposed to purely looking at the player's break point save percentages in isolation. If we were to do this, all the players at the top of the statistics would be the big servers, which would give us no edge because the market already expects them to win more service points than the average player.

ATP analysis

The best ATP players at saving break points using the formula **Break Point Save Percentage minus Average Service Point Percentage** prior to the 2014 season (stats from 2013) are shown in the table below. The mean is -2.4%.

Player	Score
Adrian Mannarino	7.6%
Martin Klizan	6.3%
Pablo Andujar	4.4%
Jesse Levine	4.4%
Janko Tipsarevic	3.9%
Dmitry Tursunov	2.9%
Ernests Gulbis	2.8%
Ryan Harrison	2.7%
Albert Montanes	2.5%
Gilles Simon	2.3%
Ricardas Berankis	2.3%
Denis Istomin	1.8%

If we were to back these players, particularly the non-notorious big servers or non-top-level players, such as Mannarino, Klizan and Andujar, we should have a positive expectation because there will be very few in the market that will anticipate that these players will be so good at saving break points against the average player.

The worst ATP players using the same formula prior to the 2014 season are shown in the table below.

Player	Score
Albert Ramos	-8.8%
Guido Pella	-8.1%
Sergiy Stakhovsky	-8.0%
Ivo Karlovic	-7.7%
Benjamin Becker	-7.6%
Michael Llodra	-7.5%
Julien Benneteau	-7.2%
Paul-Henri Mathieu	-7.1%
Juan Monaco	-7.1%

Player	Score
Igor Sijsling	-7.0%
David Ferrer	-6.8%
Alexandr Dolgopolov	-6.7%
Lukasz Kubot	-6.60%

Some of these figures are clearly very poor and are not from inconsiderable samples. Looking at these we would be able to find some great trading opportunities.

I also did the same research for the WTA.

WTA analysis

The best WTA players at saving break points using the formula **Break Point Save Percentage minus Average Service Point Percentage** prior to the 2014 season (stats from 2013) are shown in the table below. The mean is -1.9%.

Player	Score
Virginie Razzano	5.0%
Barbora Zahlavova Strycova	4.7%
Flavia Pennetta	4.0%
Tamira Paszek	3.5%
Petra Kvitova	3.3%
Mirjana Lucic-Baroni	3.0%
Lauren Davis	2.6%
Kaia Kanepi	2.6%
Andrea Petkovic	2.4%

As with the majority of the men's players, there is no way that much of the market will anticipate these players being good at saving break points. We definitely have an edge with this type of trade against the average player.

The worst WTA players with the same formula prior to the 2014 season are shown in the table below.

Player	Score
Donna Vekic	-11.6%
Monica Puig	-9.5%
Marina Erakovic	-7.6%
Olga Puchkova	-7.4%
Kirsten Flipkens	-7.0%
Monica Niculescu	-6.3%
Julia Glushko	-6.0%
Misaki Doi	-5.9%
Michelle Larcher De Brito	-5.8%
Yaroslava Shvedova	-5.6%

Of course, for balanced analysis, we also need to assess whether the receiving player is good at converting break points.

Players who are good at converting break points

ATP analysis

Obviously, as the mean for the ATP for saving break points was -2.4% compared to normal points, the mean for converting break points is 2.4% above the normal point.

The best ATP players at converting break points using the formula **Break Point Won Percentage minus Average Return Point Percentage** prior to the 2014 season (stats from 2013) are shown in the table below.

Player	Score
Jack Sock	13.2%
Nikolay Davydenko	7.8%
Michal Przysiezny	7.4%
Ivan Dodig	7.2%
Adrian Mannarino	6.8%
Alejandro Falla	6.4%
Leonardo Mayer	6.2%
Nicolas Almagro	6.0%
Aljaz Bedene	6.0%

Player	Score
Jo-Wilfried Tsonga	5.9%
Robin Haase	5.7%
Filippo Volandri	5.7%
Lleyton Hewitt	5.4%

Interestingly, Adrian Mannarino also featured on the list of top players for saving break points. It is clear that he should be a player who you can rely on more in key points than the average player.

Bad ATP players at converting break points prior to the 2014 season, using the same formula as the best ATP players, are shown in the table below.

Player	Score
Ricardas Berankis	-3.9%
Andrey Kuznetsov	-3.6%
Paolo Lorenzi	-2.8%
Guillaume Rufin	-2.8%
Victor Hanescu	-2.1%
Pablo Andujar	-2.0%
Vasek Pospisil	-1.8%
Evgeny Donskoy	-1.6%
Lukas Rosol	-1.3%
Novak Djokovic	-1.0%
Milos Raonic	-1.0%
John Isner	-0.8%
Richard Gasquet	-0.6%

It's clear that the Lithuanian Ricardas Berankis is very poor at converting break points, as he has come out on top with the lowest score in my last two samples for this data (April 2013 and October 2013).

WTA analysis

Good WTA players for converting break points prior to the 2014 seasons, using the formula **Break Point Won Percentage minus Average Return Point Percentage**, are shown in the table below.

Player	Score
Mirjana Lucic-Baroni	12.4%
Michelle Larcher De Brito	9.6%
Lucie Hradecka	9.5%
Anna Schmiedlova	8.2%
Lesia Tsurenko	6.7%
Julia Glushko	6.3%
Lara Arruabarena	6.0%
Jana Cepelova	5.9%
Kimiko Date-Krumm	5.6%
Urszula Radwanska	5.6%
Shuai Zhang	5.6%
Simona Halep	5.5%
Yanina Wickmayer	5.2%
Alison Riske	5.1%

WTA players that were bad at converting break points prior to the 2014 season, again using the same formula as above, are shown in the table below.

Player	Score
Mariana Duque Marino	-5.8%
Camila Giorgi	-3.9%
Alja Tomljanovic	-3.6%
Stefanie Voegele	-3.5%
Kristina Mladenovic	-3.1%
Maria Joao Koehler	-2.7%
Anabel Medina Garrigues	-2.6%
Yvonne Meusburger	-2.5%
Chanel Scheepers	-2.5%
Mathilde Johansson	-2.4%
Paula Ormaechea	-2.4%
Maria Kirilenko	-2.3%
Varvara Lepchenko	-2.0%
Misaki Doi	-1.9%
Teliana Pereira	-1.9%
Roberta Vinci	-1.8%

Summary

These stats should give you an overall insight into which players perform better than others in these key situations. It also should be very useful for you to be able to perform your own analysis for this in the future, if you want to keep these statistics up to date.

For me, trading break points is very simple. I stay in the trade until the game is either level at deuce or the game is won. I will never enter at 0-40 because the risk/reward ratio is very poor, and 15-40 is fairly borderline in this respect. Usually I enter and exit within one point only – entering at either 30-40 or 40-A and getting out at 40-40 or service break.

At the End of the First Set

CLEARLY, ESPECIALLY IN BEST OF THREE SET matches, winning the first set is a huge advantage as the winner only needs to win one more set to win the match.

But how much of an advantage is it?

If you did a survey of gamblers and pundits, you would probably get a variety of extreme answers from "almost guaranteed to win" to "it's just one set out of three". I don't deal in speculation so I have all the statistics necessary to gauge just how much of an advantage a first set win actually is.

WINNING AND LOSING THE FIRST SET

The results of my calculations are shown in the tables below.

WTA

Winning the first set

Starting price (SP)	Win Percentage when winning the first set	Implied odds
1.01-1.20	96%	1.04
1.01-1.50	94%	1.06
1.01-2.00	90%	1.11
2.00-2.99	77%	1.30
3.00-5.99	63%	1.59

The Win Percentage for top 100 players when winning the first set (any SP) is 87%.

Losing the first set

Starting price (SP)	Win Percentage when losing the first set	Implied odds
1.01-1.20	48%	2.08
1.01-1.50	39%	2.56
1.01-2.00	30%	3.33
2.00-2.99	15%	6.67
3.00-5.99	11%	9.09

The Win Percentage for top 100 players when losing the first set (any SP) is 22%.

Before I analyse the statistics, the eagle eyed amongst you may have noticed that the win percentage for top 100 players winning the first set is 87% but when losing the first set is 22%, and you are probably wondering why it doesn't add up to 100%. That's because sometimes top 100 players face opponents outside the top 100.

Analysis

From these statistics there are several areas that interest me. Using the midpoint of each price range (clearly this is not exact, but it should be pretty reasonable), we can say that a player that starts at 1.11 should have a price of 1.04 if they win the first set – that's pretty much spot on.

However, if that player loses the first set, would they go to 2.08? That's incredibly unlikely in my opinion. I feel that in the best of three WTA match, they'd still be odds-on after losing the first set. This situation is almost certainly due to the weight of money supporting the favourite when they are losing – it's a common entry point for many traders and is clearly illustrated in that example.

This can be further considered by the success of pre-match underdogs priced 3.00-5.99 when winning the first set. These players win on average 63% of the time, from a midpoint starting price of 4.50. Would a player starting at 4.50 be 1.59 after winning the first set? That's fairly unlikely, in my opinion. I feel that they'd probably be a bigger price than this – again lending weight to the argument that backing heavy favourites when losing is poor value due to the market forces keeping the price of the heavy favourite lower than it should be. To clarify, the market odds on the favourite will be lower than the implied odds based on their percentage chances of winning.

Therefore we can assume that backing the favourite in the WTA when a set down, applied as a blanket strategy, is a losing one. Having said that, I'm sure that used selectively it can produce a profit.

I also compiled the same statistics for the ATP.

ATP

Winning the first set

Starting price (SP)	Win Percentage when winning first set	Implied odds
1.01-1.20	99%	1.01
1.01-1.50	95%	1.05
1.01-2.00	91%	1.10
2.00-2.99	74%	1.35
3.00-5.99	61%	1.64

The Win Percentage for top 100 players when winning the first set (any SP) is 84%.

Losing the first set

Starting price (SP)	Win Percentage when losing first set	Implied odds
1.01-1.20	67%	1.49
1.01-1.50	44%	2.27
1.01-2.00	37%	2.70
2.00-2.99	17%	5.88
3.00-5.99	9%	11.11

The Win Percentage for top 100 players when losing the first set (any SP) is 25%.

Comparative analysis of WTA and ATP

As we can see from comparing the WTA stats with the ATP stats above, favourites clearly enjoy a bigger advantage in the men's game than they do in the women's when winning the first set. However, overall we see that the women generally win more matches when a set up, due to the increased win percentages for underdogs.

The two underdog price brackets in the ATP had a lower average win percentage than for the WTA – so men's favourites tend to be able to come back and win in three sets more often than women's favourites. The statistics on losing the first set back that up – men priced from 1.01 to 1.20 come back on average 67% of the time, which is a huge increase on the women's 48%. Not only that, but the win percentage at the starting price 1.01-1.50 was bigger for the men (44% against 39%), and it was too for the price 1.01-2.00 (37% against 30%).

I personally consider that men's favourites tend to come back more than women's because of the bigger gap in fitness amongst male players, and to some extent mental strength. I truly believe that a great deal of tennis is played in the mind. Some players are very, very weak in the mental strength department and also lack fitness, particularly in the third set. These deficiencies will prevent them from reaching the levels that their ability warrants. If you see a player who is strong or weak mentally or physically, make a note of that. This knowledge could earn you a lot of money in the future.

FIRST SET SCORELINE

Another factor that influences the market price after the first set is the scoreline of the first set. Logically, many people consider that the player that enjoys the bigger advantage in the first set should be so dominant that the second set is a mere formality.

However, that isn't necessarily the case. We saw a prime example of that in the French Open quarter final on 4 June 2013.

Serena Williams started her quarter final match with Svetlana Kuznetsova as heavy favourite at 1.07. She dominated Kuznetsova in the first set, winning it 6-1. Only the extremely optimistic Kuznetsova fan would expect Kuznetsova to be able to turn the match around but she almost managed it, taking the second set 6-3 and leading 2-0 in the third set. Kuznetsova actually traded as slight favourite at around 1.80 at that point. Clearly even with extremely heavy favourites winning the first set by a dominant margin, winning the match is far from a formality.

So, as usual, several years ago I decided that having an opinion wasn't enough and decided to investigate the statistics further. I sampled a large number of men's and women's matches, with any starting price and player rank considered, and obtained the results shown in the following tables.

ATP

First set score	Match Win Percentage
6-0	92%
6-1	86%
6-2	86%
6-3	86%
6-4	79%
7-5	84%
7-6	76%

WTA

First set score	Match Win Percentage
6-0	97%
6-1	89%
6-2	90%
6-3	81%
6-4	83%
7-5	77%
7-6	79%

From these statistics, we can see that generally the closer the first set score the lower the success rate is for winning the match, with there generally being a drop from the 6-0 to 6-3 scoreline in the ATP to the 6-4 to 7-6 scorelines, and the 6-0 to 6-2 scorelines in the WTA to the 6-4 to 7-6 scorelines.

If we notice an overreaction in the market after a close set, especially in situations where a player gets broken at *5-6 or loses a tight tiebreak, we can often obtain good value because clearly in those situations the match win percentage for the first set winner will be at the lowest possible figures.

PLAYER'S RECORD WHEN A SET UP OR SET DOWN

Another area we can look at when the first set is completed is a player's record when a set down or up. Some players have a strong negative mentality when they drop the first set, whereas it inspires others to come back. Some players get complacent when they drop the first set, or lack self belief that they can win. It's important to know which players fall into the various categories.

Below you will find analysis and stats for this area for the ATP and the WTA.

ATP

The Australian legend Rod Laver had the highest career win percentage a set down, winning an incredible 48.4% of matches from that point. Out of the current players, Rafael Nadal's 42.1% is the highest, and unsurprisingly he and the other current top three players make up the top five current players over the career stats, along with Lleyton Hewitt.

However, Hewitt's inclusion here clearly shows the danger of looking at career stats. His career is on the wane and you can argue the same for Roger Federer to some extent as well. I prefer to look at the 12-month stats for match situations, personally.

The 12-month stats, correct prior to the 2014 season, are shown in the tables below.

GOOD PLAYERS WHEN A SET UP

Player	Match Win Percentage
Rafael Nadal	100%
Novak Djokovic	97%
Tommy Robredo	97%
Albert Montanes	95%
Andy Murray	94%
Kei Nishikori	94%
Milos Raonic	94%
Juan Martin Del Potro	93%
Nicolas Almagro	92%
David Ferrer	91%
Jo-Wilfried Tsonga	91%
Stanislas Wawrinka	91%

Jeremy Chardy, Alejandro Falla, Roger Federer, Robin Haase, Andrey Kuznetsov, Paul-Henri Mathieu, Vasek Pospisil and Gilles Simon all had Win Percentages of 90% when a set up.

BAD PLAYERS WHEN A SET UP

Player	Match Win Percentage
Martin Klizan	44%
Grega Zemlja	57%
Aljaz Bedene	59%
Marcos Baghdatis	59%
Evgeny Donskoy	61%
Horacio Zeballos	63%
Daniel Gimeno-Traver	69%
Leonardo Mayer	71%
Igor Sijsling	72%
Adrian Mannarino	72%
Michael Llodra	73%
Lukas Lacko	73%

Sergiy Stakhovsky, Juan Monaco, Victor Hanescu, David Goffin and Ivan Dodig all had Win Percentages of 74% when a set up.

From these stats we can see which players thrive when a set up and which have a lot more difficulty converting a set advantage into a match win. Whilst it's worth noting that many of those ATP players with good records a set up are top players, it's not exclusively the case.

Clearly the list of players above who have bad records a set up will give you an idea of who it could be viable to lay when a set up. It's very interesting to see that Martin Klizan was the worst ATP performer when a set up with a 44% win rate – this is by some distance the worst record that I've ever seen. I have never once seen a negative record when a set up (Klizan is 8-10 in 2013 when a set up), so this information cannot be ignored. Assuming the market isn't fully aware of this, opposing the Slovak when he is a set up appears mandatory.

What is also useful is to see which players do well when a set down, and which players tend to wave the white flag in those situations. Again, the tables below show 12-month stats correct at June 2013.

GOOD PLAYERS A SET DOWN

Player	Match Win Percentage
Andy Murray	60%
Novak Djokovic	59%
Rafael Nadal	59%
Juan Martin Del Potro	46%
John Isner	41%
David Ferrer	39%
Marin Cilic	38%
Dmitry Tursunov	38%
Stanislas Wawrinka	36%
Roger Federer	35%
Richard Gasquet	35%
Ernests Gulbis	35%
Lleyton Hewitt	35%
Jo-Wilfried Tsonga	35%

BAD PLAYERS A SET DOWN

Player	Match Win Percentage
Paul-Henri Mathieu	5%
Andrey Kuznetsov	5%
Julien Benneteau	5%
Radek Stepanek	7%
Lukas Lacko	7%
Lukas Rosol	8%
Paolo Lorenzi	8%
Albert Ramos	9%
Michael Llodra	9%
Victor Hanescu	9%
Alejandro Falla	9%
Alexandr Dolgopolov	9%
Yen-Hsun Lu	11%
Evgeny Donskoy	12%
Juan Monaco	13%
Adrian Mannarino	13%
Ryan Harrison	13%
Albert Montanes	14%
Leonardo Mayer	14%
Lukasz Kubot	14%
Daniel Gimeno-Traver	14%
Nikolay Davydenko	14%

Edouard Roger-Vasselin, Marinko Matosevic, Ivo Karlovic, Jeremy Chardy and David Goffin all had a Win Percentage of 15% when a set down.

Whilst it's definitely fair to say that most of the above players who perform badly when a set down are at the lower end of the ATP tour, there are some notable higher-level players in this sample. The likes of Jeremy Chardy, Juan Monaco, Julien Benneteau, Radek Stepanek and Nikolay Davydenko are much more illustrious names than most on the list. It would be wise to be cautious about backing these players when they are losing.

WTA

The results of the same research for the WTA are shown in the tables below. Again, these are 12-month stats correct at June 2013.

GOOD PLAYERS WHEN A SET UP

Player	Match Win Percentage
Maria Kirilenko	100%
Yvonne Meusburger	100%
Sara Errani	98%
Victoria Azarenka	97%
Serena Williams	97%
Agnieszka Radwanska	96%
Bojana Jovanovski	95%
Kaia Kanepi	95%
Maria Sharapova	95%
Alexandra Cadantu	94%
Simona Halep	93%
Mona Barthel	91%
Sorana Cirstea	91%
Madison Keys	91%
Na Li	91%
Sabine Lisicki	91%
Elina Svitolina	91%

BAD PLAYERS WHEN A SET UP

Player	Match Win Percentage
Heather Watson	60%
Anabel Medina Garrigues	61%
Tsvetana Pironkova	63%
Andrea Hlavackova	65%
Olga Govortsova	65%
Francesca Schiavone	68%
Olga Puchkova	71%
Mandy Minella	71%
Petra Martic	71%

Player	Match Win Percentage
Julia Goerges	72%
Lourdes Dominguez Lino	72%
Laura Robson	74%
Varvara Lepchenko	74%
Johanna Larsson	74%
Annika Beck	74%
Yaroslava Shvedova	76%
Karolina Pliskova	76%
Flavia Pennetta	77%
Su-Wei Hsieh	77%
Dominika Cibulkova	77%
Yanina Wickmayer	78%
Christina McHale	78%

As with the ATP, many of the players with a good record a set up are top 20 players. However, it's worth noting that Meusburger, Jovanovski, Cadantu and Svitolina are much lower ranked and I'd be dubious about opposing them when they take the first set.

Some of the women's records when they are leading by a set are horrific. Gamblers in particular speculate about some female players' mental strength – the phrase *mental midget* is often used – and these statistics provide some evidence of this.

GOOD PLAYERS WHEN A SET DOWN

Player	Match Win Percentage
Serena Williams	75%
Victoria Azarenka	47%
Petra Kvitova	45%
Simona Halep	42%
Jelena Jankovic	42%
Roberta Vinci	38%
Stefanie Voegele	38%
Kirsten Flipkens	36%
Bojana Jovanovski	35%

Player	Match Win Percentage
Caroline Wozniacki	35%
Karin Knapp	32%
Anastasia Pavlyuchenkova	32%
Andrea Petkovic	32%

Eugenie Bouchard, Sorana Cirstea, Alize Cornet, Lauren Davis and Maria Kirilenko all had Win Percentages of 30% when a set down.

BAD PLAYERS WHEN A SET DOWN

Player	Match Win Percentage
Julia Goerges	5%
Varvara Lepchenko	5%
Kristina Mladenovic	5%
Tsvetana Pironkova	5%
Elina Svitolina	8%
Maria-Teresa Torro-Flor	8%
Misaki Doi	9%
Sara Errani	9%
Romina Oprandi	9%
Urszula Radwanska	9%
Lesia Tsurenko	10%
Timea Babos	11%
Kimiko Date-Krumm	11%
Lucie Safarova	11%
Su-Wei Hsieh	12%
Mona Barthel	13%
Irina Begu	13%
Ekaterina Makarova	13%
Karolina Pliskova	13%
Venus Williams	13%
Madison Keys	14%
Christina McHale	14%
Monica Niculescu	15%
Shuai Zhang	15%

Player	Match Win Percentage
Kiki Bertens	16%
Olga Govortsova	16%
Andrea Hlavackova	16%
Anabel Medina Garrigues	16%
Shuai Peng	16%
Jie Zheng	16%

Considering the average for winning the match when a set down in the WTA is 22%, some of these figures are as horrific as the figures regarding win percentage when a set up. There would have to be huge value offered to want to back a player on this list when a set down.

Again, there are several top players on the list – Makarova, Barthel, Errani, Safarova, Williams and Keys all have a decent reputation and in some cases their name will guarantee a short price in the market, even when losing. If they start as heavy favourite, which they often do, and their price is around evens or a little bigger when a set down, it's hard to justify backing them on the basis of these statistics.

STAKING

The final thing we need to consider at the end of the first set is our **staking**. If, for some reason, we decide to back the winner of the first set, this is slightly less of a concern because there will be a point during the second set or third set where we can at least get some of our stake back.

However, if we lay the winner of the first set and then they take the lead in the second set, or get close to winning it, we have a problem because their price will be very short – hence leading to a large percentage loss of our stake. This is less of a problem if we have laid the winner of the first set at a very low price already, as our risk is much smaller compared to our reward. However, if a heavy underdog wins the first set and we decide to lay them, we have a bigger problem.

For example – a heavy favourite starting between 1.20 and 1.25 loses the first set. Their price will, at that point, generally be around the 2.00 mark, give or take a few ticks either way. If you back them at this price, and the second set goes on serve, with no breaks, to a scoreline like 4-4, and the favourite gets broken, you are in severe danger of losing almost all your stake if you trade out when the underdog is serving for the match at *5-4.

Whilst having a high level of risk isn't necessarily a problem to experienced traders or those with a high risk tolerance, it's vital that all traders, especially novices, are aware of the potential implications. As I mentioned previously – favourites that lose the first set do not always come back! This is something that in-play gamblers definitely need to bear in mind if they decide to take a longer-term position at the end of the first set.

SINGLES PLAYERS THAT ALSO PLAY DOUBLES

One thing I've noticed from watching a lot of tennis, and doing a great deal of analysis, is that sometimes singles players don't put in maximum effort when a match isn't going easily for them when they have doubles commitments. I can only presume it's because they are aware they have these other commitments and therefore aren't too worried if they lose, or because they are tired from having to play two tournaments at the venue.

Either way, I set about assessing the records of top 50 doubles players that are top 100 players in singles as well, to see whether there was any substance in these thoughts. I did this for the ATP and WTA, as ever.

Analysis of top doubles and singles players

ATP

Just to remind readers, the average ATP Win Percentage for top 100 players when a set down is 25% and (as we will see in the next chapter) the average ATP Win Percentage for top 100 players in a deciding third set is 55%.

As usual, all win percentages are for the 12 months to June 2013.

Player	Win Percentage when a set down	Win Percentage in deciding third set
Marcel Granollers	20.00%	69.23%
Radek Stepanek	13.33%,	50.00%
Fernando Verdasco	5.26%	44.44%
Lukasz Kubot	19.23%	44.44%
Jurgen Melzer	29.41%	76.47%
Ivan Dodig	12.50%	38.89%
Julien Benneteau	18.18%	18.75%
Fabio Fognini	28.95%	50.00%
Michael Llodra	6.67%	30.00%
Rajeev Ram	25.71%	75.00%
Simone Bolelli	26.09%	83.33%
Edouard Roger-Vasselin	23.08%	51.85%

From this sample of 12 players, we can see that most players do indeed struggle in these situations. Eight of the 12 players had a below average record when a set down, and the same number had a below average record in deciding sets.

Only Jurgen Melzer, Rajeev Ram and Simone Bolelli had a positive record in both scenarios, although it's important to note that some of those wins for all three players were in Challenger Tour matches.

The means of the sample were also interesting to analyse. The average when a set down was 19.03% and the deciding set win percentage was also below average at 52.70%. It's clear to me that overall men's doubles players definitely have at least some element of decline when a set down or in deciders.

As always, it's important to treat each player on their individual merits, but a blanket strategy of opposing players in this situation (or not backing them when previously inclined to) should be worthwhile.

Note on Fernando Verdasco

It's fascinating to see the parallels between the decline of Fernando Verdasco's singles ranking (from top 10 player several years ago to current ranking of 53) to the improvement in his doubles ranking (now number

5). Perhaps that's a natural consequence of age – he is now getting towards 30 – or it could be just a reassessment of priorities, knowing that he can no longer compete at his best in singles, so is moving his focus towards doubles.

WTA

Many top 100 singles players in the WTA were ranked in the top 50 for doubles, so I cut down the sample to the top 25 doubles players.

Again, to remind readers, the average WTA win percentage for top 100 players when a set down is 22%, and the average WTA win percentage for top 100 players in a deciding third set is 55%.

Player	Win Percentage when a set down	Win Percentage in deciding third set
Sara Errani	14.29%	63.16%
Roberta Vinci	25.93%,	58.62%
Nadia Petrova	31.58%	60%
Andrea Hlavackova	18.18%	50%
Lucie Hradecka	10.53%	44.44%
Ekaterina Makarova	17.39%	43.75%
Elena Vesnina	25%	68.75%
Maria Kirilenko	22.73%	60%
Su-Wei Hsieh	13.64%	50%
Kristina Mladenovic	9.09%	60.87%
Jie Zheng	20%	63.16%
Shuai Peng	25.00%	60%
Lucie Safarova	14.81%	53.33%
Bethanie Mattek-Sands	15.79%,	57.14%

The decrease in doubles players' abilities in adversity in the singles matches was less pronounced for the women than the men, although there was some decrease, particularly for players when a set down. Nine of the 14 players were below the 22% average, with the mean for the 14 players being 18.85%. However, there was no correlation between women's doubles players and deciding set records – with the mean here being 56.66%, marginally above the WTA top 100 average of 55%.

From these statistics, we can infer that there appear to be cases where female doubles players put less than full effort into matches when a set down, but when it comes to a deciding set they appear to be fully competitive.

The Deciding Set

THE DECIDING SET WILL ALWAYS BE THE MOST volatile set for tennis trading, with extreme price movements for breaks and even holds of serve. This is clearly logical because the match is reaching its conclusion and this set decides the winner.

The effect of this is that these price movements mean a very high percentage loss of stake when trades go against you. Of course, this works the other way too, with very high percentage gains when trades go for you, but I wanted to make novice traders aware of the extra risk in this set.

There are several prevalent trends that the market usually exhibits at the start of a deciding set.

PREVALENT TRENDS AT THE START OF A FINAL SET

Firstly, unless the winner of the second set was a heavy favourite, the winner of the second set is almost always a shorter price than their starting price. Not necessarily by much, but the market does factor in the momentum of winning the second set at the start of the third set.

Secondly, based on the first point, a heavy favourite will almost always be a bigger price than their starting price at the beginning of the third set, with a pronounced difference if they lost the second set.

I don't necessarily agree with the first condition. In my experience I've found that the deciding set is a lot more random than the market thinks.

I did a detailed sample of both ATP and WTA matches and found that the average win percentage for players that win the second set to equalise the match at one set all was 53% for both tours. Clearly there is only a very slight advantage with regards to momentum for winning the second set.

DECIDING SET PRICE RANGE STATS

Here are some deciding set price range statistics:

ATP

Starting price (SP)	Win Percentage	Implied odds
1.01-1.50	71%	1.41
1.01-2.00	66%	1.52
2.00-2.99	45%	2.22
3.00-5.99	33%	3.03

The Win Percentage for the top 100 players is 55%.

WTA

Starting price (SP)	Win Percentage	Implied odds
1.01-1.50	67%	1.49
1.01-2.00	61%	1.64
2.00-2.99	43%	2.35
3.00-5.99	38%	2.63

The Win Percentage for the top 100 players is 55%.

Analysis

What we can see here is that the ATP favourites win slightly more than the WTA favourites in the final set, and therefore there is a clear advantage for WTA underdogs over ATP underdogs.

Furthermore, if we compare the implied odds to the midpoints of each starting price band (not perfect, but this should be a reasonably accurate guide) we can see why the price on a favourite will be higher than the starting prices at the start of the deciding third set.

Because there are only tiny effects of momentum, I just trade the third set considering the merits of each player. I also bear in mind that the second set winner may well be priced too short in the market, and therefore there may be some value on the player that lost the second set.

So effectively what I am looking at in deciding sets are several things.

THINGS I LOOK FOR IN DECIDING SETS

Firstly, as always, I trade according to my projected hold model, knowing which players are good or bad servers, and may be undervalued by the market in this regard.

Secondly, I'm looking for fatigue in players and this is especially applied with regard to those players with poor deciding set records.

PLAYERS WITH GOOD AND BAD RECORDS IN DECIDING SETS

The tables below show the good and bad performers in deciding sets in the 12 months to June 2013. As I mentioned before, the average percentage for top 100 players in both the ATP and WTA was 55%.

ATP

PLAYERS WITH GOOD DECIDING SET RECORDS

Player	Win Percentage
Rafael Nadal	88.89%
Feliciano Lopez	84.62%
Kei Nishikori	84.62%
Simone Bolelli	83.33%
Jurgen Melzer	76.47%
David Ferrer	75.00%
Rajeev Ram	75.00%
Novak Djokovic	73.33%
Florian Mayer	72.73%

Player	Win Percentage
Paolo Lorenzi	72.22%
Grigor Dimitrov	71.43%
Marcel Granollers	69.23%
Marin Cilic	69.23%
Lleyton Hewitt	68.75%

As we can see, the list of ATP players who have strong deciding set records is quite mixed. There are the top two players in the world – Rafael Nadal and Novak Djokovic, as well as top five player David Ferrer. However after that, just Kei Nishikori, Grigor Dimitrov and Marin Cilic are ranked around the top 20.

Lleyton Hewitt's success is no surprise, as it goes along with his career statistics. He is (correctly) often noted for his warrior qualities.

What this sample of players illustrates is that individual player tendencies – such as fitness – are much more important than ranking or ability in deciding sets.

PLAYERS WITH BAD DECIDING SET RECORDS

Player	Win Percentage
Alexandr Dolgopolov	16.67%
Julien Benneteau	18.75%
Martin Klizan	29.41%
Michael Llodra	30.00%
Go Soeda	33.33%
Jeremy Chardy	35.71%
Ivan Dodig	38.89%
Juan Monaco	40.00%
Marcos Baghdatis	40.00%
Paul-Henri Mathieu	41.18%
Nikolay Davydenko	41.67%
Sergiy Stakhovsky	42.42%
Albert Ramos	43.75%
Carlos Berlocq	43.75%
Pablo Andujar	43.75%

Player	Win Percentage
Fernando Verdasco	44.44%
Lukasz Kubot	44.44%

No top 20 ATP players were in the list of players with poor deciding set records.

Alexandr Dolgopolov (who has suffered from a fatigue related illness), Ivan Dodig, Juan Monaco and Fernando Verdasco are the highest ranked players and generally those in the list are not the stronger members of the ATP Tour.

WTA

PLAYERS WITH GOOD DECIDING SET RECORDS

Player	Win Percentage
Maria Kirilenko	83%
Stefanie Voegele	78%
Sorana Cirstea	76%
Simona Halep	76%
Kaia Kanepi	75%
Johanna Larsson	75%
Yvonne Meusburger	75%
Victoria Azarenka	73%
Jamie Hampton	71%
Maria Sharapova	71%
Serena Williams	71%
Sloane Stephens	71%
Elena Vesnina	71%
Alexandra Cadantu	70%
Agnieszka Radwanska	69%
Kirsten Flipkens	68%

It's also worth noting that Lara Arruabarena (who did not play the required 25 matches for inclusion in the sample) was 7-0 – 100% – in deciders in 2013.

What can be seen here is that half of the top 10 in the WTA are represented in the above table – Halep, Azarenka, Sharapova, Williams and Radwanska. Furthermore, players ranked around the top 20 – Kirilenko, Stephens, Vesnina and Flipkens – also feature.

With only Johanna Larsson and Alexandra Cadantu being ranked outside the top 50, it can be said that a strong deciding set record is generally something only higher ranked players achieve.

PLAYERS WITH BAD DECIDING SET RECORDS

Player	Win Percentage
Shuai Zhang	0%
Anabel Medina Garrigues	17%
Tsvetana Pironkova	22%
Polona Hercog	25%
Lucie Hradecka	25%
Misaki Doi	29%
Yaroslava Shvedova	29%
Julia Goerges	31%
Kimiko Date-Krumm	33%
Su-Wei Hsieh	33%
Christina McHale	33%
Flavia Pennetta	33%
Monica Puig	33%
Varvara Lepchenko	35%
Ekaterina Makarova	36%
Heather Watson	36%
Kiki Bertens	36%
Andrea Hlavackova	36%
Karolina Pliskova	38%
Maria-Teresa Torro-Flor	38%
Ana Ivanovic	38%
Lucie Safarova	40%
Lesia Tsurenko	40%
Galina Voskoboeva	40%

Break Back Percentages

USING MY ULTIMATE IN-PLAY SPREADSHEETS, I HAVE calculated break back percentages based on the time decay of the set and break back stats, for both the ATP and WTA. I provide analysis of the data for the two tours in turn in this section.

The time decay of the set is measured by the amount of games expired immediately after the break lead occurs. The break back stats are measured by adding the percentage likelihood that the relevant player loses a break lead in a set to the percentage likelihood that their opponent recovers a break deficit in a set (all stats derived from my Ultimate In-Play Spreadsheet).

ATP

Being able to estimate the percentage chances of a break back occurring in a set is a very valuable asset because it enables us to be on the right side of many swing trading opportunities. Especially in the ATP, an initial break lead reduces a player's price in-play significantly, and a break back will return the price to a similar level to where the price was before the break occurred. The data below was derived from the period 1 July 2013 to 15 October 2013.

For the ATP, the break back stats are then broken down into five categories:

* Sum of Under 50.00

* Sum between 50.00 and 59.99

* Sum between 60.00 and 74.99

* Sum between 75.00 and 89.99

* Sum Over 90.00

The average percentage chance of a top 100 player giving a break lead up was 32.14% and the percentage chance of getting a break deficit back was 35.42% (this is higher due to the fact that they play players outside the top 100). This means the average sum can be considered to be 67.56% – almost the midpoint of the third, middle category of the five above. We can also then assume that the average percentage chance of a break back occurring in ATP matches is 33.78% (67.56%/2).

As we can see in the tables below, the stats based on the combined sum of the two players show a huge trend towards the higher percentages.[1]

When the two players' combined score is under 50, breaks were broken back on 22.49% of occasions, and this barely rises when the combined score is between 50 and 59.99, where breaks were broken back on 22.81% of occasions. It is clear from this data that laying the player a break up in this scenario has a very low chance of success – 11.29% and 10.97% below average respectively.

Whilst readers may think this is fairly obvious, and would occur when top players are a break up, it also occurs in a great variety of other scenarios. For example, the likes of Philipp Kohlschreiber and Janko Tipsarevic have atrocious stats for getting a break deficit back and many of their matches would have been included in these two categories.

It's interesting to see that with the average break back percentage being 33.78% in the ATP, the break back stats for the middle bracket – 60.00 to 74.99 – were almost exactly average (as mentioned previously, the midpoint is almost exactly the combined average) giving 34.66% of break backs.

The break back stats greatly increase when looking at the 75.00 to 89.99 and over 90 combined scores – with break backs occurring on 40.63% and 43.75% of occasions respectively in these brackets.

---

1 The tables are also available from my website: ATP link: www.tennisratings.co.uk/resource--break-back-stats-by-time-decay-break-back-stats; WTA link: www.tennisratings.co.uk/wta-break-back-percentages-based-on-time-decay-break-back-stats

Considering time decay

Up to game six

We can also see from the table below that break backs occur at different percentages based on the time decay of the set (games completed).

An average player that breaks in either the first or second game of the set has a slightly above 40% chance of getting broken back – just under 7% above average – and that is unsurprisingly the highest percentage for expired time due to the player having more time to defend his break lead.

However, the percentage from game three to game six is fairly consistent and around average (36.98% dropping to 31.37%) so it can be considered that when the combined score is high and the break lead occurs on or before game six of the set, the break recovery will occur on average just under 50% of the time.

When a break back occurs more than half the time

There are also circumstances where the break back will happen more often than 50% – which should provide us with great opportunities for laying the player a break up.

These occur when the players' combined break back score is over 75 and the break occurs in the first or second game of the set (e.g. to produce a score of *1-0 or 2-0*). We can see from the stats below that in this scenario the break back occurred 85 out of the 147 times sampled (57.82% of the time).

Game eight or game nine

Going back to the percentages by time decay, we can see that from game eight or later, the percentages for the break back drop markedly. A break after game eight of a set will generate a *5-3 scenario, and after game nine will generate a *5-4 scenario, so the player who has just obtained a break lead will be serving for the set immediately.

It appears that laying the player a break up in these situations is not a viable proposition because there is just a 10.75% chance of a break back in the *5-3 case and a 14.13% chance of a break back in the *5-4 case.

These percentages are well below the current ATP average for breaking opponents (21.5%), showing that players serving for the set hold more often than average.

My research for this area in the WTA found similar below average figures. Players getting broken serving for the set obviously does happen but because gamblers and traders remember these instances more vividly than an early lead – because of the *choke* factor, because it has a huge influence on the position of the match, and especially due to the popularity of discussing this phenomenon on social media – the gambling public appears to think it happens more often than it actually does.

The 11th game of the set

It's worth noting the phenomenon of the 11th game of the set. In the data I observed, 17 break backs occurred in 65 instances (26.15%) of a player breaking for a *6-5 advantage.

There could be several reasons for this – firstly the sample size isn't the biggest (I will add to all these stats when I have more data in the future). Secondly it could be because the set is closer than other scenarios and will often feature players more evenly matched on that basis. Finally, it could also be because the server feels under more pressure to hold serve because it's a one shot chance of winning the set. At *5-3 or *5-4, for example, he knows that even if he gets broken he will still have another shot at his opponent's serve.

Based on my research, it's clear that combining time decay and the break back data will generate many positive expectation opportunities for profit. If you laid the player blindly a break up when the combined score was over 75, you'd have had 427 entry points in the three and a half months sampled, and would have had 176 winning trades (41.22%). In the vast majority of those trades your profit would be significantly higher than your potential loss.

The complete data can be seen below. Please also note the key following the tables.

BREAK AFTER GAME 1 OF SET

Combined Score	Back On Serve		Break back %
	Yes	No	
<50	11	34	24.44
50-60	16	43	27.12
60-75	50	72	40.98
75-90	39	32	54.93
90+	11	6	64.71
Overall break-back percentage for this game in the set			40.45

BREAK AFTER GAME 2 OF SET

Combined Score	Back On Serve		Break back %
	Yes	No	
<50	6	15	28.57
50-60	14	35	28.57
60-75	30	52	36.59
75-90	28	18	60.87
90+	7	6	53.85
Overall break-back percentage for this game in the set			40.28

BREAK AFTER GAME 3 OF SET

Combined Score	Back On Serve		Break back %
	Yes	No	
<50	7	23	23.33
50-60	9	19	32.14
60-75	34	44	43.59
75-90	16	25	39.02
90+	5	10	33.33
Overall break-back percentage for this game in the set			36.98

BREAK AFTER GAME 4 OF SET

Combined Score	Back On Serve		Break back %
	Yes	No	
<50	9	18	33.33
50-60	4	23	14.81
60-75	22	39	36.07
75-90	14	27	34.15
90+	2	1	66.67
Overall break-back percentage for this game in the set			32.08

BREAK AFTER GAME 5 OF SET

Combined Score	Back On Serve		Break back %
	Yes	No	
<50	5	15	25.00
50-60	6	22	21.43
60-75	14	26	35.00
75-90	13	15	46.43
90+	2	6	25.00
Overall break-back percentage for this game in the set			32.26

BREAK AFTER GAME 6 OF SET

Combined Score	Back On Serve		Break back %
	Yes	No	
<50	3	15	16.67
50-60	4	7	36.36
60-75	15	26	36.59
75-90	9	20	31.03
90+	1	2	33.33
Overall break-back percentage for this game in the set			31.37

BREAK AFTER GAME 7 OF SET

Combined Score	Back On Serve		Break back %
	Yes	No	
<50	3	13	18.75
50-60	5	13	27.78
60-75	12	27	30.77
75-90	7	15	31.82
90+	2	4	33.33
Overall break-back percentage for this game in the set			28.71

BREAK AFTER GAME 8 OF SET

Combined Score	Back On Serve		Break back %
	Yes	No	
<50	2	11	15.38
50-60	0	18	0.00
60-75	3	29	9.38
75-90	5	22	18.52
90+	0	3	0.00
Overall break-back percentage for this game in the set			10.75

BREAK AFTER GAME 9 OF SET

Combined Score	Back On Serve		Break back %
	Yes	No	
<50	0	9	0.00
50-60	2	13	13.33
60-75	3	32	8.57
75-90	4	22	15.38
90+	4	3	57.14
Overall break-back percentage for this game in the set			14.13

BREAK AFTER GAME 11 OF SET

Combined Score	Back On Serve		Break back %
	Yes	No	
<50	1	9	10.00
50-60	0	10	0.00
60-75	9	15	37.50
75-90	6	10	37.50
90+	1	4	20.00
Overall break-back percentage for this game in the set			26.15

OVERALL BREAK BACK PERCENTAGES

Combined Score	Back On Serve		Break back %
	Yes	No	
<50	47	162	22.49
50-60	60	203	22.81
60-75	192	362	34.66
75-90	141	206	40.63
90+	35	45	43.75

Key:

* **Break After Game x of set** = A player leads by a break immediately after that game of the set

* **Combined Score** = The sum of the % the relevant player loses a break lead in a set added to the % their opponent recovers a break deficit in a set (all stats derived from the Ultimate In-Play Spreadsheet).

WTA

As mentioned for the ATP, being able to estimate the percentage chances of a break back occurring in a set is a very valuable asset because it enables us to be on the right side of many swing trading opportunities. An initial break lead reduces a player's price in-play significantly, and a break back will return the price to a similar level to where the price was before the break occurred. The data was derived from August 1st, 2013 until the end of the Tournament of Champions in Sofia, on November 3rd, 2013.

The break back stats for the WTA are broken down into the following five categories:

* Sum of Under 75.00

* Sum between 75.00 and 89.99

* Sum between 90.00 and 104.99

* Sum between 105.00 and 119.99

* Sum Over 120.00

The percentages in 2013 for a top 100 (and a few notable others) WTA player, according to the stats on the **Ultimate In-Play Spreadsheet** were as follows:

The average for giving a break lead up was 47.87% and for getting a break deficit back it was 50.25% (this is higher due to the fact that they play players outside the top 100), so the average sum can be considered to be 98.12%. This is almost the midpoint of the third, middle category. We can also then assume that the average percentage in WTA matches for a break back to occur is 49.06% (98.12%/2).

As we can see based on the tables below, the stats based on the combined sum of the two players show a huge trend towards the higher percentages, which is similar to the ATP.

When the two players' combined score is **under 75**, there have been break backs just 15.63% of the time, which is well below the expectation of around 30-35% (there were very few combined scores below 60% and most were around the 70% region in this bracket).

When the combined score is between **75 and 89.99**, and **90.00 and 104.99** the break back figures were almost identical (46.60% and 46.54% respectively). These figures were somewhat surprising considering the sample size was fairly decent in these areas.

Considering the midpoint of each bracket is effectively double the expectation for the figures, we can see that the 75-90 bracket overachieved. The midpoint expectation was 41.25% for this bracket so we can see the actual results indicated just over 5% more break backs than expected.

The 90.00 to 104.99 bracket had a midpoint expectation of 48.75%, so we can see that the actual results were slightly below expectation – 2.21% below the expected figure.

With all areas having below the average break back percentage, it would not be recommended to lay a player a break up when the combined score of them giving up a break lead and their opponent recovering a break deficit is under 105. This would be particularly the case if projected holds were also above average.

As I detailed in the ATP analysis, at this point many readers may think this is fairly obvious, and would occur when top players are a break up. However, it also occurs in a great variety of other scenarios. For example, the likes of the highly-rated **Eugenie Bouchard** and top 20 player **Kirsten Flipkens** (both often start matches as a strong favourite) have very poor stats for getting a break deficit back. There are also some lower-ranked players with strong break deficit recovery percentages.

The break back stats greatly increase when looking at the two brackets over 105.

The **105.00 to 119.99** bracket showed a dramatic increase from the 90.00 to 104.99 bracket, with break backs occurring 58.90% of the time (12.36% above the 90.00 to 104.99 bracket). This was also slightly above the midpoint expectation of 56.25%. We can see with this large increase that situations are much more in our favour, with us now more likely to have a profit from our trade than a loss when we lay the player a break up in the set.

The final bracket, which comprises match-ups with **over 120.00 combined score**, had a fairly small sample but had very similar results to the 105.00 to 119.99 bracket, with a break back percentage of 58.46%. It's worth mentioning that my expectation for this over 120.00 bracket was around 62-63%. I can't remember there being many (if any) match-ups with a combined score over 130.

We can see from the tables below that break backs occur at different percentages based on the time decay of the set (games completed).

Considering time decay

Compared to the ATP data, the WTA data for time decay is much less pronounced. The ATP data showed there was a big discrepancy between the start and end of sets, with there being 40.45% and 40.28% break backs when the break lead was obtained in the 1st or 2nd game of the set, compared to 10.75% and 14.13% when the break lead was obtained in the 8th or 9th game of the set.

However, the WTA data was less stark, with there being just a 22.89% difference between the highest and lowest game percentages (1st game of the set = 58.33%, 7th game of the set = 35.44%). The ATP largest difference was 29.70%.

An average player that breaks in either the first (58.33%) and second (47.54%) games of the set has exactly a combined 54% chance of getting broken back – just under 5% above average. Unsurprisingly that's the highest percentage for expired time due to the player having more time to defend her break lead.

However, I will reiterate the point that the percentage decreased much less than I expected with time decay and laying the player a break up when the break comes in the latter stages of sets appears much more viable in the WTA than in the ATP.

Circumstances with a high chance of a break back

There are some circumstances where there is an **extremely high chance of a break back occurring**.

When the combined score is over 105, and the break lead originated in the first or second game of the set, the player a break down got the set back on serve 71.97% of the time (95/132). Furthermore, when the combined score went over 120, whilst the sample size was small, the player a break down got the set back on serve 84.21% of the time (16/19).

These situations provide us with some **very high expectation** opportunities for laying the player a break up.

For the ATP I spent some time discussing the phenomenon of the 11th game of the set. In the ATP, when the break came in the 11th game of the set (so a player is *6-5 up) the break back came much less than expectation, and I discussed the reasons behind that.

This was not the case in the WTA, with the break-back percentage being 37.50%. This is pretty much exactly the same as the average WTA service break across all surfaces of 36.70%, so this appears to be a trend that only applies for the ATP.

How can we use this data?

Based on my research, it's clear to see that combining time decay and the break back data provided in the **Ultimate In-Play Spreadsheet** will generate many positive expectation opportunities for profit. If you laid the player blindly a break up when the combined score was over 105, you'd have had 357 entry points in the three months sampled, and 210 winning trades (58.82%). This figure is well above the average break-back percentage of 49.06%.

We can also look to the set betting markets – if the data indicates there is an above average chance of a break back, we can look to back the player a break down to win the set, often at a big price.

Finally, I want to mention a **social experiment** I did using Twitter. I asked for some estimates for a break back percentage for the following situation and asked for some reasons as to why:

> A WTA player that recovers a break deficit on 60% of occasions goes *1-0 down to a player that loses a break lead 55% of the time.

I wanted to get a handle on what people's perceptions were, both for the percentage and for the reasons why – a bit of a market sample, if you like.

Not one reply mentioned the time decay of the set (or it being at its lowest point) and the average of the Twitter sample was 57.8%. The highest estimate was 80%, and the lowest 33%.

We can see from the data below that the figure from my sample was around 71.43% from the 105.00 to 119.99 combined score bracket (the sample had a 115 combined score – not far from the midpoint of that bracket).

This experiment also lends weight to the fact that the market expects the break back to occur less than it actually does – which is exactly what we want and need for this type of trade to show a long-term profit.

The complete data can be seen below. Please also note the key following the tables.

BREAK AFTER GAME 1 OF SET

Combined Score	Back On Serve		Break back %
	Yes	No	
<75	0	5	0.00
75-90	44	35	55.70
90-105	70	63	52.63
105-120	50	20	71.43
120+	11	2	84.62
Overall break-back percentage for this game in the set			58.33

BREAK AFTER GAME 2 OF SET

Combined Score	Back On Serve		Break back %
	Yes	No	
<75	2	11	15.38
75-90	18	30	37.50
90-105	41	49	45.56
105-120	29	14	67.44
120+	5	1	83.33
Overall break-back percentage for this game in the set			47.5

BREAK AFTER GAME 3 OF SET

Combined Score	Back On Serve		Break back %
	Yes	No	
<75	1	0	100.00
75-90	18	18	50.00
90-105	42	32	56.76
105-120	29	19	60.42
120+	5	4	55.56
Overall break-back percentage for this game in the set			56.55

BREAK AFTER GAME 4 OF SET

Combined Score	Back On Serve		Break back %
	Yes	No	
<75	1	4	20.00
75-90	20	11	64.52
90-105	25	30	45.45
105-120	16	14	53.33
120+	3	3	50.00
Overall break-back percentage for this game in the set			51.18

BREAK AFTER GAME 5 OF SET

Combined Score	Back On Serve		Break back %
	Yes	No	
<75	0	2	0.00
75-90	11	13	45.83
90-105	35	23	60.34
105-120	10	1	90.91
120+	5	3	62.50
Overall break-back percentage for this game in the set			51.69

BREAK AFTER GAME 6 OF SET

Combined Score	Back On Serve		Break back %
	Yes	No	
<75	0	3	0.00
75-90	8	14	36.36
90-105	17	26	39.53
105-120	9	15	37.50
120+	3	2	60.00
Overall break-back percentage for this game in the set			38.14

BREAK AFTER GAME 7 OF SET

Combined Score	Back On Serve		Break back %
	Yes	No	
<75	0	0	N/A
75-90	4	10	28.57
90-105	15	27	35.71
105-120	6	7	46.15
120+	3	5	37.50
Overall break-back percentage for this game in the set			35.44

BREAK AFTER GAME 8 OF SET

Combined Score	Back On Serve		Break back %
	Yes	No	
<75	0	1	0.00
75-90	6	13	31.58
90-105	11	20	35.48
105-120	7	3	70.00
120+	0	2	0.00
Overall break-back percentage for this game in the set			38.10

BREAK AFTER GAME 9 OF SET

Combined Score	Back On Serve		Break back %
	Yes	No	
<75	0	1	0.00
75-90	10	10	50.00
90-105	11	27	28.95
105-120	10	7	58.82
120+	3	4	42.86
Overall break-back percentage for this game in the set			40.96

BREAK AFTER GAME 11 OF SET

Combined Score	Back On Serve		Break back %
	Yes	No	
<75	1	0	100.00
75-90	5	11	31.25
90-105	9	18	33.33
105-120	6	5	54.55
120+	0	1	0.00
Overall break-back percentage for this game in the set			37.50

OVERALL BREAK BACK PERCENTAGES

Combined Score	Back On Serve		Break back %
	Yes	No	
<75	5	27	15.63
75-90	144	165	46.60
90-105	276	317	46.54
105-120	172	120	58.90
120+	38	27	58.46

Key:

* **Break After Game x of set** = A player leads by a break immediately after that game of the set.

* **Combined Score** = The sum of the % the relevant player loses a break lead in a set added to the % their opponent recovers a break deficit in a set (all stats derived from the Ultimate In-Play Spreadsheet).

Dangerous Situations

In trading, as we have discussed before, as our full stake is usually a lot bigger than our maximum tolerable loss, a loss of a full stake is disastrous. Traders need to ensure that this does not happen – they must guard against situations that can possibly manifest themselves which make this a possibility.

PLAYER RETIREMENTS

The situation where you will lose your full stake is when the player that you have backed retires. Betfair rules are that if a player retires before the first set is completed, all bets/trades are voided. However, if a player retires after the first set is completed, all bets stand. If you have a large liability on a player and they retire, that's a horrific prospect.

There's no real way to predict when a player is going to retire, apart from watching the matches to see if a player's movement is restricted. Even then it's not a given you will be able to tell in advance of a retirement, as players often get injured mid-point.

However, there's one way we can protect ourselves, to some extent.

Protecting yourself against player retirements

The most common time for a player retirement is immediately after the first set. Perhaps some players are just as aware of most bookmaker rules as the gamblers.

So, for example, if we have laid a player at some point in the first set but the trade goes against us and the player we have laid goes towards winning the set, it's wise to get out just before the end of the set, at a score such as 40-0 or 40-15, to protect our stake and get as much out of a losing trade as we possibly can.

Also, if we want to back the player that has lost the first set and there is some hint of an injury for them in the first set, we should wait until it is obvious they are not going to retire in the break between sets before we back them.

Examples of player retirements

Even taking precautions, at some point you are going to get burned by a retirement. Thankfully they are pretty rare but they do happen. Andy Murray even retired immediately after winning a second set tiebreak against Marcel Granollers in May 2013. I heard several horror stories on Twitter of traders backing Murray when he won the tiebreak, only to look on in horror as he immediately retired, leading to them losing their whole stakes.

I got burnt in the match between Kirsten Flipkens and Julia Goerges in April 2013. Goerges took the first set 6-2 but, as we have noted, she has a poor record when a set up. Flipkens has an excellent record a set down, so it appeared to be a viable trading opportunity, with Goerges starting the second set at around 1.2.

Flipkens, at the end of the first set, received a medical timeout so I decided to wait until she held serve before laying Goerges, in case Goerges raced away with the second set. She held serve, then Goerges held serve for 2-1. Flipkens immediately retired. Thankfully my risk wasn't huge as I laid at a very low price, but it was still a very nasty loss.

Medical timeouts

Medical timeouts are an interesting facet of the game that requires some explanation. Tennis players can request a medical timeout for non-serious injuries at the end of sets or a change of ends. If a player injures themselves more seriously mid-point, such as turning an ankle or pulling a muscle, they can request an immediate medical timeout.

The market very often overreacts to a medical timeout. It's not that uncommon for a player's price to move from underdog to under 1.20 or even lower when their opponent has a medical timeout.

It's very hard to back the *non-injured* player because there are many other people trying to do the same thing – so with the five-second delay factored in the price you try and get matched at is usually gone and your bet is unmatched.

I tend to look at it from another perspective. In many cases, the player with a medical timeout continues playing. Sometimes they will retire, but very often they do not. If a player falls a very large number of ticks – to below 1.2 or, even better, below 1.1 – following their opponent's medical timeout, then I will look to lay the *non-injured* player. At those prices it is a very low-risk proposition.

If the *injured* player starts playing and appears even slightly competitive, that price will rise back towards where the price was before the medical timeout. I've seen instances before where a *non-injured* player was 1.1x following the medical timeout, then their *injured* opponent comes back from the timeout and wins the next point and then the *non-injured* player's price goes up to over 1.5.

Timeouts in the WTA

I'm particularly cynical of medical timeouts, especially in the WTA, so this tactic works very well for the women. As I previously mentioned, the market often overreacts to a medical timeout, despite the fact that often – especially in the WTA – the player isn't genuinely, or severely, injured. Medical timeouts are often perceived by cynics such as myself to be *tactical timeouts*, but the market almost always overreacts to them, fearing a potential retirement.

Victoria Azarenka gained notoriety in the Australian Open in January 2013 when she requested a medical timeout during her semi-final against Sloane Stephens. After blowing five match points whilst serving for the match at 5-3, Azarenka immediately requested a medical timeout when she was broken. Stephens had to wait ten minutes to serve at *4-5, and was promptly broken to lose the match. Many watchers felt Azarenka requested the timeout to recover some composure, although she did claim to have a rib injury.

If you're on the wrong end of a medical timeout because a player you have backed calls it, it can be a very painful experience and there's very little to recommend to try and avoid the situation or to minimise the damage, except trying (often in vain) to get a fair bit of your stake back. A higher risk approach is to hope that the timeout is called for an aforementioned frivolous reason and on resumption of play the market will move back towards normal. However, if you enter the market following a medical timeout, the experience can be the opposite, especially in the WTA.

THE GAME BEFORE A POTENTIAL TIEBREAK

Another dangerous situation, which isn't as dangerous as retirements but is still worth mentioning, is the game before a potential tiebreak.

Let's say that you decide to lay a player when they are serving at *5-6 in a set. However, they then hold serve and it goes to 6-6 – and to a tiebreak. The tiebreak starts pretty much immediately following the last point of the previous game and if you can't get your exit trade matched quickly before the start of the tiebreak you could be in a worse position if the first point of the tiebreak also goes against you. Of course, it could work in your favour too, but that would be pure gambling. And that's what we are trying to avoid.

Dealing With Losing Positions

We all get losses. It's unavoidable. Even the best trader in the world can lose on a match, lose over a day, almost definitely lose occasionally over a week and sometimes may even lose over a whole month or longer. When edges are reasonably small and variance is high, that's the nature of the game.

However, what makes successful traders different to less successful ones is the way they deal with losses. A successful trader will shrug off a loss because they know they made the right moves with higher expected value than the market price, but got unlucky.

A less successful trader tends to take the loss much more to heart, either fearing that their strategy (which may be solid) is flawed or, even worse, they go *on tilt* and chase their losses, losing more money gambling on other matches where they may have no edge. Even worse still, they may gamble on negative expectation games such as roulette, blackjack, slots or FOBTs (fixed odds betting terminals) in bookmaker's shops.

When our first trades go against us in a match, it's easy to get downhearted and feel that the match is going to be a big loss. Some traders decide to cut their losses at this point, which is fine *if* they feel that a bigger loss will begin to affect them psychologically. However, as long as their strategy is sound, they are mathematically making a mistake, as each trade should be treated separately to the last one and effectively they are mutually exclusive of one another.

I've heard statements before similar to "when you're up on a market, play with the profit only, so you guarantee yourself profit on the match". This is a hugely flawed approach because you are losing theoretical expected value on your future trades by trying to protect your profit. It's definitely not an approach I advocate.

Averaging down

A fairly risky approach that can provide the opportunity to get you out of trouble is **averaging down**. The theory behind this strategy is that you **average down** the price of your lays on a player so that you only need a few ticks movement in your favour to exit a previously losing position at either break even, or maybe even profit.

This example should illustrate what I mean.

A player takes the first set and is trading at 1.40. You decide that you want to lay the player at this point and lay him for £100, giving you a liability of £40 (£100*0.40).

However, this player soon breaks and leads *3 1. Let's just assume that at this point his price is 1.10. If we hedge our position equally our loss on each player would be £27.27.

If we decide not to do this, but instead add to our position further, we **average down** our average lay price. If we add to our position by laying for £300 at 1.10, giving us an extra liability of £30, our total liability would now be £70.

BUT – our average lay price has moved from 1.40 at the start of the first set, to 1.175 (our £70 liability divided by £400 potential profit). All we would need to break even, therefore, is a 7.5 tick movement in our favour – from the current price of 1.1 out to 1.175 – at some point in the rest of the match.

You can mess around with the numbers more, if you are so inclined. If you want to lay for a bigger amount, incurring a bigger liability, at situations like the 1.10 price I mentioned above, then you will need even less of a tick movement to reach your break-even point. For example, if you lay a further £600 at 1.10, giving the extra liability of £60 instead of the £30 previously, our average lay price is now around 1.14 (£100 liability divided by £700 potential profit).

This style of trading isn't for everyone, but it's worth considering, especially when there is still plenty of potential time left in the match, like the example I gave above.

Psychology, Risk and Bankroll Management

How much to risk on a trade

Personally I'm very risk averse. So by that I mean that I hate taking risks more than most. For me, protecting my trading bank is absolutely key. I will not do anything which will jeopardise my trading bank, or a significant proportion of it. There are a number of factors that I need to consider when calculating a viable amount to risk on a given trade, so that I don't over-stake and risk great damage to my bank.

When I used to do pre-match betting only, I was also very cautious with my risk. I'd only risk a maximum of 3% of my betting bankroll on a given bet. I see so many phrases online, full of bravado, such as "full bank on her!" or "I'm huge on him!" and this is the wrong mentality. Of course, these characters may or may not be full bank or huge on a player – that's the risk you take when you listen to others on social media (perhaps another book could be written just on those dangers!).

Whilst with a cautious management of bankroll you only accumulate growth in a slower way, it's the most secure way of doing so. Unless your strategies or prices on each player are flawed, you will earn money. Who won the race? The hare or the tortoise?

I'll only risk a maximum of about 8% of my trading bank on an individual trade. I do personally feel there's scope for this to be a little larger, around 10-12%, but I wouldn't want to risk any more than that.

When I say 8%, it's important to clarify that. I will possibly add to that, if I want to **average down** my average lay price, but the biggest position I've taken has been a liability of about 11% of my trading bank.

It's important to clarify this still further by saying that I won't trade such a high percentage in the most volatile situations that occur in matches, such as tiebreaks or deciding sets. That percentage would be a first set trade, where a lot of the sting has already been taken out of the price of the player I wish to lay.

Also I need to say that I would never let this whole sum be risked by letting a trade run in its entirety. I'm in and out relatively quickly. I ensure that the biggest loss that can occur is around 2.3% of my trading bankroll in any one trade.

Stop-losses

There's been a lot written on the necessity to have stop-losses. It's not necessarily required in a lot of scenarios. When people say stop-losses, usually they mean they get out when their loss figure hits a certain point. This doesn't necessarily interest me, because my trades tend to have that built in.

I'll use a (very) rough example.

Two players start at evens. One player breaks and leads *4-3 in the first set. His price, depending on a few factors, will be roughly around the 1.5 mark. If he holds his serve twice and wins the set, say 6-4, in all likelihood his price will be 1.25-1.3. If you know you're getting out at the end of the set, you have your stop loss built in automatically – if you lay the leader at 1.5 and you know you will trade out if the player a break down doesn't get the break back, that's your stop loss. So if you lay the leader at 1.5 for £50 liability, and he holds, if you then back the same player at 1.3 for £115.38 at the end of the set, your equal red on either player is £15.38.

So automatically you are restricting your loss to just over 30% of your liability. It's a simplistic example, and the prices for the scenarios may not be spot on as they're hugely situational, but you should understand what I mean. As long as you know your potential downside, and are fine with that amount because it's a small percentage of your bankroll, then you are in a good position.

To execute these sort of trades obviously requires discipline. I'm sure most readers have been tempted to hold on to losing positions for a little longer than they perhaps felt they should. Doing so puts your bankroll at much higher risk. Every single successful gambler or trader needs discipline – without discipline you are nothing, no matter how talented you are at reading matches, programming systems, whatever. There's no shame at all in exiting with a red position if the trade goes against you.

As I mentioned previously, obviously you will need to let some trades run, such as in a final set or if you're laying a player a set and a break up in the second set, but by staking less in these scenarios you can clearly still control your losses to a manageable amount.

Mental stability

One thing that's very hard to do is to maintain mental stability, but it's key. There is nothing wrong with going out and leaving the rest of the matches if your head isn't all there. To use a poker phrase, if you are *on tilt* just turn your computer off.

People seem split on profit-taking. By that I mean when you're having a huge day, do you just turn the laptop off and bank your profit? Or are you leaving expected value behind doing that? Theoretically I suppose you are. But if your mental state is going to be better for future days if you bank that profit and finish for the day then maybe that is the best thing to do. I don't think there's an exact answer for that one. Do what suits you best.

Just remember that as soon as your emotions start to get the better of you, turn the computer off.

As long as you show discipline, have solid, consistent strategies based on the right reasons and control your losses then there's no reason that you can't make good money trading tennis.

As I mentioned earlier, if you are just starting to trade, there's no reason why you need to start big. Start with trades just for several pounds and see how you get on. If you stake small but your strategies are flawed, you'll only lose a small amount. Staking more doesn't mean you'll win more often, it will just multiply your losses.

Resources

I would recommend using the following resources when doing your tennis trading research:

* **www.tennisinsight.com** – subscription required – excellent statistic-based tennis community.

* **www.atpworldtour.com** – good range of statistics for the men's tour (much better than the equivalent WTA website for this) in the 'FedEx Reliability Zone' area.

* **www.tennisbetsite.com** – excellent tennis statistics website including point by point scoring information for all past matches.

* **www.oddsportal.com** – the best range of available bookmakers' prices and also provides past pricing data on the 'Results' tab.

If you are interested in projected holds and the effect that knowing these for every match could have on your trading, I would highly recommend subscribing to my **TennisRatings Daily Spreadsheet**.

With **Tier One** subscriptions working out as cheap as 83p per day when taking out a three-month subscription, and **Tier Two** subscriptions (including rolling projected holds and break back percentages for each player daily) at £1.38 per day on the same basis they represent excellent value for money.

The spreadsheet provides projected hold percentages for every ATP and WTA match, as well as my model price for each match, and a break point *clutch* score which shows how successful each player should be saving break points based on both players' break point scores, relating them to the ATP/WTA means.

The **Ultimate In-Play Spreadsheet** shows a players' service hold percentages for early and late stages of sets, as well as break back percentages for every player in the top 100 (and a few more notable players as well), plus set win percentages for each player in every set.

If you have any questions about any part of this handbook, please feel free to email me at **tennistrades@gmail.com**. I will get back to you as quickly as possible.

Milton Keynes UK
Ingram Content Group UK Ltd.
UKHW021334260924
448888UK00011B/229